NOTES FROM THE TALKING DRUM

Exploring Black Communication and Critical Memory in Intercultural Communication Contexts

THE HAMPTON PRESS COMMUNICATION SERIES
Communication, Globalization and Cultural Identity
Jan Servaes, series editor

The Dao of the Press: A Humanocentric Theory
 Shelton A. Gunaratne

Connectivity, Networks, and Flows: Key Concepts for Contemporary
 Media and Cultural Studies
 Andreas Hepp, Friedrich Krotz, Shaun Moores
 & *Carsten Winter* (eds)

Notes from the Talking Drum: Exploring Black Communication and
 Critical Memory in Intercultural Communication Contexts
 Mark C. Hopson

Viewing the South: How Globalisation and Western Television
 Distort Representations of the Developing World
 Emma Miller

Cultural Citizenship and the Challenges of Globalization
 Wenche Ommundsen, Michael Leach & *Andrew Vandenberg* (eds.)

Media and Power on the Margins of Europe: The Public Negotiation
 of the Breton Language and Cultural Identity
 David P. Winterstein

forthcoming

New Voices Over the Air: The Transformation of South African
 Broadcasting in a Changing South Africa
 Eric Louw and Viola Milton

Picturing Afghanistan: The Photography of Foreign Conflict
 Paul Verschueren

Serbian Spaces of Identity: Narratives of Belonging by the Last
 "Yugo" Generation
 Zola Volcic

NOTES FROM THE TALKING DRUM

Exploring Black Communication and Critical Memory in Intercultural Communication Contexts

Mark C. Hopson
George Mason University

 HAMPTON PRESS, INC.
CRESSKILL, NEW JERSEY

Printed in the United States of America

Library of Congress Cataloging-in-Publication Data

Hopson, Mark C.
  Notes from the talking drum : exploring black communication and critical memory in intercultural communication contexts / Mark C. Hopson.
     p. cm. -- (Hampton Press communication series, communication, globalization and cultural Identity)
  Includes bibliographical references and indexes.
  ISBN 978-1-61289-004-3 (hardbound) -- ISBN 978-1-61289-005-0 (paperbound)
  1. African Americans--Communication. 2. African Americans--Race identity. 3.
Intercultural communication--United States. 4. Communication and culture--United States. 5. African Americans in mass media. I. Title.
  P94.5.A372U5558 2011
  302.2089'96073--dc22
                                                    2010051722

Hampton Press, Inc.
23 Broadway
Cresskill, NJ 07626

For Danielle, Romere, and Autumn
—Love, Enjoy, Protect, and Support

CONTENTS

FOREWORD

"As If It Were True..."

Ronald L. Jackson II

*University of Illinois–
Urbana Champaign*

Cultural identities are messy. They come equipped with signifiers that slip and slide, multiply and hide, and find themselves always in question, under close scrutiny. It is not that it is any one person's fault that they are so messy, but that our society does not release us from the obligation to vigilantly observe and experience the effects of cultural difference.

In Mark Hopson's book *Notes From the Talking Drum,* he brings to bear questions of racial and cultural identity. Immediately, readers are introduced to the vitality of the talking drum in African Diaspora societies. As much as he explicates the drum as a communication instrument, he also informs us of its transformative rhetorical power. Hopson invokes a sense of urgency about what we must do, understand, appreciate, and value about the talking drum. Explaining that the talking drum is essentially a way in which Hopson himself has been invited to rethink his own sense of cultural personhood, he also reminds us that the talking drum is a signpost for critical memory, cultural history, and the basic ingredient of all communication—the word.

What we learn in this nuanced text is that the word alone is insufficient. Not only do words limit the imagination by confining reality into consumable bits of information, but words are also symbols operating in a sociolinguistic context. The meanings applied to words vary according to who's expressing and receiving them when, how, why, and how. This is an important point to make because both the content and style of the writing in this book come to us as "notes," which is a form that seeks to disabuse us of any notions we have about linear writing. In fact, in the Afrocentric tradition, one might call his writing style *curvilinear*. So, in many ways, Hopson exemplifies a form and structure that covers much terrain in a volume that could be double or triple its size. Its conciseness forces us to grapple with the concepts in a way we wouldn't if we had to read twice or three times as much material. Yet, I don't want to overcelebrate the brevity in lieu of discussing this book's value.

Rather than repeat the fetishization of difference that has become so popular in contemporary diversity texts, Hopson interrogates current discursive practices like a film director showing the audience a pastiche of lived experiences operating in different social conditions beginning with his own experience as a graduate student being introduced to a radio show on Black culture. We quickly learn that culture is first and foremost personal. Oftentimes, people talk about culture as institutional, but it is at the personal level that we experience it daily, in living our lives. The lens Hopson explores most is his own African ancestral identity, and he unabashedly discusses African-centered Black communication principles, ideas, and paradigms.

African centered theorizing merges in chapter 2. Hopson insists that we question knowledge production and circulation. He implores that we thoughtfully consider how we have been domesticated by a pedagogy that has disinvested itself from multiculturalism. He asks that we query what is natural and how it got to be that way. If epistemological singularity is what intoxicates and entrances us, Hopson presumes a responsible, culturally centered paradigmatic turn is the elixir that will make us sober.

Hopson passionately argues that a society that is bereft of honor and civic integrity becomes inhibited by its own fractures. It cannot move forward; it cannot become socially progressive when its relational, political, and social foundations remain hampered. It is the "Black Gaze," as chapter 3 calls it; this reminds me of Chris Rock's recent movie *Black Hair*. Rock says he developed the movie to try to answer his daughter's questions about her own beauty. For too long, Blacks have been objects of specular subjectivity and have had to deal with the psychological baggage of not having their humanity affirmed in a country that they helped to build. The gaze, as Kobena Mercer suggests, lands squarely on those for whom cultural difference is a socially manufactured problem. Hopson contends that Black children find themselves socially abandoned via racist practices at an early age. They are taught that their worth is tied up in their ability to act White, look White, speak White, and be White, knowing all along that they are Black. Obviously this statement requires a complex examination of what this means.

More specifically, what I understand Hopson to say in this book is that Black life in the United States remains ever complicated by persistent and seemingly ubiquitous racism. How else do we explain racial profiling, police brutality, as well as disproportionate unemployment, under-education, under-insurance, under-representation, and poverty of Blacks as an aggregate population in virtually every sector of U.S. society? Put quite plainly, racism is a social problem that has invaded Black lives. Blacks have tried to think it away. Blacks have worked hard through community social action, personal initiative, and life-protecting protests to fight it away. Blacks have developed conceptually sophisticated rationales concerning their want for celebration of all humanity without exception in order to appeal to nonmarket sense of love, caring, and ethics. We rationalize that things are getting better and that the Black middle class has expanded. We prop up the indelible image of Barack Obama being inaugurated as U.S. President to remind ourselves we can do this too, in this still-racist society, and more importantly to remind ourselves that the American Dream is designed for all Americans, not just Whites. Even as we work against systemic oppression while coaching ourselves that nihilism is not the answer, we work hard to overcome racism and its debilitating effects. *Notes of a Talking Drum* implores us as Americans to collectively work hard to institutionally and individually redress racism and its concomitant effects.

I am reminded of my own experience as a Black male growing up in Cincinnati, Ohio. I experienced my first episode of racism at the age of 7. Racism has reared its ugly head many more times throughout my life up to now. Each time, I was left feeling that perhaps it was something I did. After I realized it wasn't my fault, surprisingly I didn't feel any more relieved. In fact, I felt emotionally paralyzed because I couldn't control the racist behaviors launched against me. I realized I could only control how I interpreted and felt about those incidences. I could only control how I would proceed. I could only control the degree to which I allowed racism to inhibit my success. Despite all we have learned and been taught about race and racism Blacks and other marginalized groups are often left "holding the bag" for all the negativity that racism produces, so we teach ourselves that we shall overcome and we use the metaphorical talking drum to uplift one another.

We should write a book that consists of articles on the various aspects of Black communication. . . . This book should be of use to students and teachers and others interested in understanding the various problems and issues.

—Jack L. Daniel, May 25, 1970,
Open letter to the Black Caucus
of the Speech Communication Association

PREFACE

It is not simply I think therefore I am, but rather that I am related and relate to others, therefore I am.

—Karenga (2003, p. 17)

The objective of this book is to increase understanding about the ways in which persons of African descent living in the United States (i.e., Black/African Americans) witness a dynamic intercultural experience. Orators, communicators, authors, scholars, and artists have documented a long history of Black–White communication. To this end, I draw from selected texts to highlight rhetorical challenges and strategies for Black/African American communicators within predominantly White/ European American societal structures.

Traditional models suggest that communication is made up of several components, including senders, receivers, messages, channels, and situations. Within most models, noise obstructs the flow of communication. As such, we might also define noise as a psychological construct which consists of (mis)perceptions of race and culture—including social, political, and historical forces—that impact our intercultural and interracial interactions. In other words, our inner thoughts can and will influence our interactions with other people. This book works to foreground the "intercultural and interracial noise" by aligning, superimposing, and knotting together stories about a complex communication process— Black communication within predominantly White social structures.

I begin this book by situating Black communication as part of a unique intercultural/interracial experience. Within my analysis, the Black experience is forged in stories about Black life. These include the autobiographical, semi-autobiographical, and fictional works that encapsulate distinct challenges and success for Black communicators. I have found that communication of the past often mirrors communication of the present. For example, Barack Obama's famous 2008 speech, "A More Perfect Union," drew from themes in the Preamble to the United States Constitution. This proved to be beneficial strategy when the presidential candidate needed it most. (According to the Pew Research Center, approximately 85% of U.S. citizens listened to at least some portion of the speech.) Indeed, voices of the past contribute to a synoptic story about race and culture, and merit the attention of scholarship today.

As another point, I examine specific tensions for Black communicators within predominantly White societal structures. For example, some Blacks describe their interactions as oscillating between good–bad, visible–invisible, voice–voiceless, and empowered–disempowered when attempting to communicate as nondominant group members. In strategic response to these tensions, Black communicators may silence themselves in the presence of Whites, confront Whites, work to gain trust from Whites, and work to educate Whites about co-cultural issues. Within my analysis, these tensions and strategies occur across rhetorical dimensions of gaze, voice, and space.

Finally, I foreground some African American rhetorical traditions that express, represent, and transform Black life. The Black experience has been explored eloquently in classic texts and narratives which are based in principles of African American rhetoric. For example, Black authors overwhelmingly employ nommo—the power of the spoken and written word—to name, define, resist, and articulate life throughout periods of slavery, the Reconstruction era, and the Civil Rights Movement. This rhetorical creativity is evident today, throughout all areas of social life—including politics, business, health, and entertainment. African American rhetorical traditions demonstrate great value for history, affirmation and possibility, discursive formations of space and freedom, profound optimism, imperatives to overcoming racism, and the human journey overall.

PRIMARY TEXTS

Black Boy, Invisible Man, and *Bone Black* are metaphors that carry tacit meaning for Black Americans today. Originally released in two parts, *Black Boy: A Record of Childhood and Youth* is the autobiography of Richard Wright. Here, Wright remembers coming of age in the segregated American South, and speaks to the struggles of Black men living in a society that renders them powerless as though they were children. He journeys North in search of humanity, but finds that communicative tensions seem only to take new forms and fashion.

Ralph Ellison's semi-autobiographical *Invisible Man* is another prolific observation of racial interactions. Ellison's depiction of Black manhood as "invisible" within predominantly White structures grew to become a popular metaphor throughout the 20th century. After revisiting Ellison's introspective account, I suggest that Black manhood remains largely invisible within predominantly White America. As the result of disproportionate incarceration and miseducation, Black men continue to face threats of being minimized, mischaracterized, and altogether omitted from larger society.

In *Bone Black*, bell hooks interrogates race and gender roles. She recalls growing up in the American South where Black womanhood is a unique and sometimes stifling cultural experience. The lessons learned will later prove to be the foundation of her scholarly activity. For example, her children's book *Happy to be Nappy* highlights the imagistical constructions of beauty and self-esteem that impact Black girlhood. Indeed, hooks joins Wright and Ellison to give insight to the secret worlds of marginalized individuals and groups. Their critical memories add to the breadth and depth of an intercultural project which I base on two overarching criteria: (1) the narrative's potential for thick description around various thoughts, ideas, and memories of the Black experience, and (2) the narrative's capacity to situate the Black experience within an intercultural or interracial context.

Undoubtedly, numerous accounts speak to Black experiences. I do not claim to include all perspectives here. There are multiple truths further espoused in books like *Incidents in the Life a Slave Girl*; *Narrative of Sojourner Truth*; *Narrative of the Life of Frederick Douglass: An American Slave*; *Coming of Age in Mississippi*; *The Autobiography of Malcolm X*; and *Assata*—just to name a few. These and other works contribute directly and indirectly to my own talking drum. As authors we each tell a different story. Together we are responsible for constructing a more truthful world. The collective effort inspires me to strive for an intellectual program once described by Thomas Kochman (1981) as lending to emancipation from racism, social oppression, and cultural subordination.

There is little doubt that intercultural communication can be a precarious and contradictory concept to theorize. Again, I make no claims to speak for or about all people. Nor do I mean to infer identity for all individuals and groups. I understand that life is much more complex than mere generalizations. My exploration is meant to add to discourse concerning marginality within the intercultural experience. At the very least, I hope this book will strengthen the reader's awareness concerning the ways in which culture, race, power, and difference impact communication within a diverse society.

ORGANIZATION OF THE BOOK

This book is comprised of six chapters. Chapter 1 positions Black communication as an intercultural experience. To illustrate the point, I consider Black communication suffusing the 2008 presidential election and foreground ways in which race and culture is framed through discourse. Chapter 2 presents the African-centered principles, intercultural communication research, and power and privilege theories that create the impetus for my talking drum. Additionally, chapter 2 introduces critical memory as a rhetorical means for capturing and interpreting distinct Black communication practices. Chapter 3 begins discussion on primary themes, including the iterativity of racism occurring within the Black gaze. Chapter 4 presents voice as a primary theme created and practiced by Black communicators. Chapter 5 presents the theme of rhetorical and racialized space. Also, within chapter 5, I examine gaze, voice and space as they have applied to my own academic and intercultural interactions. Chapter 6 concludes the book with a critical discussion, and limitations and heuristic value in this area of communication research.

One

CONCEPTUALIZING
THE TALKING DRUM

In some traditional African societies [writing and speaking] have been admirably satisfied by the drum. Communication was swift and the range was great; in the event that the first drummer was unable to reach all the necessary persons, another drummer, at the outer fringes, could take up the message of another transmission. The drummer along with the village sage became a repository of all the historical data relating to the village.

—Asante (1998, p. 71)

In this section, I situate intercultural communication as I have come to understand it. First, I invite the reader to engage my African-centered approach—that is, my talking drum—and to see Black/African American communication as part of a unique intercultural interaction. Next, I suggest that critical memory adds depth and clarity to a communicative experience grounded in expression, resistance, and transformation of

Black life. Finally, I introduce tension and strategy, and speculate on ways in which racism becomes a rhetorical phenomenon that impacts intercultural communication of the past and present.

MY TALKING DRUM

The talking drum begins with the rich cultural history of African people. The African drum is an instrument used to celebrate, tell stories, and share information. It is tradition, legendary, and rhetorical. It is a form of communication. This book is my talking drum; with it I take up and extend transmissions to villages near and far. Asante (1998) notes that African American culture represents developments in African culture and history inseparable from place and time. Indeed, the African drum is linked to the experiential, historical, and multidimensional journey of African people. The drum activates collective and critical memories about the Black experience.

Inspiration for my talking drum is also credited to a New York radio show dedicated to Black culture. As a graduate student in a predominantly White region of southeastern Ohio, I would listen to cassette recordings (a testament to another historical medium) of "The Talking Drum" sent by my father who received them from a family friend. During this critical time in my life, the radio show, the recordings, and the two elders all helped to keep me informed. As you can see, the African drum includes broad based concepts of Black communication.

Central to my talking drum is *nommo*—which suggests that everything begins with the word. Powerful words introduce new thoughts and ideas. Nommoic creativity is the foundation for contemporary Black communication that is fresh, innovative, creative, and stretches for meanings not necessarily captured within established bounds of English language (Gray, 2001; Karenga, 2003). Our words articulate life's journey. Descendants of Africa have always relied on spoken and written words to represent, express, and transform life. For example, 19th century slave narratives worked in multiple ways to (a) document the conditions of slavery, (b) call for efforts to end slavery, (c) impart religious inspiration, (d) affirm identity, (e) redefine what it means to be Black, (f) make money, and (g) inform the audience. Slave narratives written before the Civil War describe the horrors of enslavement, whereas post-Civil War narratives emphasize the benefit and the challenges of emancipation (Taylor, 2005).

Classic literature has much to say about intercultural communication. We must acknowledge these voices to better understand life today. African-centered principles justify the use of classic works. For example, *harmosis* emphasizes the synthesis of ancient and traditional culture with contemporary culture (Asante, 1998; Gray, 2001; Karenga,

2003). Consider hip-hop music wherein human drumming informs computerized drumming, and the art of human beat-boxing meets the digital rhythms of drum programs. Harmosis intertwines the past and the present. It is based in the historic works of great artists, writers, and thinkers. Given the breadth and depth of great ideas, their texts gain relevance over the years. Classic expressions illustrate a particular vantage-point—Equiano, Douglass, Truth, and Du Bois—all observe and explore human interactions. Their prolific thoughts withstand the tests of time and merit attention in scholarship today.

Great literature appeals to the imagination and emotion of readers. Profound narratives form a living discourse that invites the audience to vicariously experience unknown worlds. Descriptive stories disclose life beyond one's own time and place. Introspection creates richer representation of humanity. The Black experience has been promoted, initiated, and imparted through a wide mixture of stories. All of these memories contribute to my talking drum.

The power of the written word is especially important to groups whose standpoints have been underrepresented and misrepresented in dominant culture. African classical thought has gone largely unrecognized because the imposition of the European-line-as-universal has hindered cultural understanding and demeaned humanity for non-Europeans (Asante, 1998). Recognizing the hegemonic forces that work against Black culture, my metaphoric talking drum refutes the notion of a discontinued history or uncertain future. To the contrary, I join scholars who assert that African American rhetoric is not dead, but serves as an architectonic functioning art which continuously refashions the sounds and symbols of its people.

Black communication is a unique form of intercultural communication and grounded in expression, resistance, and transformation of life. This book analyzes the words of authors who add depth and clarity to that unique experience. The works of Ralph Ellison, Richard Wright, bell hooks, and others contribute to social transformation. The commitment to consciousness-raising is evident in the stories produced by each. As such, I place collective critical memory within intercultural contexts to explore the following questions:

1. How does Black/African American communication within the United States become a distinct intercultural communication experience?
2. What are some basic truths of communication as expressed in the critical writings of Black/African American communicators, and what tensions and strategies are associated with these truths?
3. How is the Black/African American experience expressed, resisted, and transformed through language?

SITUATING BLACK COMMUNICATION AS
INTERCULTURAL EXPERIENCE

> In this country the two most extreme types of the world's races
> have met, and the resulting problem as to the future relations of
> these types is not only of intense and living interest to us, but
> forms an epoch in the history of mankind.
>
> —W. E. B. Du Bois (1897/2004, p. 19)

The Black presence in North America became a cogent intercultural experience in 1619, when Jamestown, Virginia took part in the Trans-Atlantic slave trade that would grow to involve millions of human beings (Bennett, 1968). The African Diaspora (also called *Maafa* or the African Holocaust) stripped its victims of significant cultural practice and forced conformity to dominant societal hierarchies. Consequently, African survival strategies included acculturation and submission to dominant ways. Today, the desire for survival, approval, acceptance, and progress compels descendants of Africa and other nondominant group members to enact practices and values associated largely with White/European American culture. For these reasons, Black communication as intercultural communication is a necessary discussion.

The complexities surrounding Black–White communication are comparable to other intercultural and interracial interactions. Yet Black–White communication is a process unique unto itself. If, as mechanistic models suggest, noise impedes the communication process, then one may argue that Black–White communication within the United States has been informed by the entropic rumblings of slavery, Jim Crow, segregation, discrimination, and institutionalized racism (Delgado & Stefancic, 2001; Odih, 2002).

Of course individuals and groups learn to interpret racialized phenomena in multiple ways. Undoubtedly, we all hold different truths. This chapter makes no attempt to ignore the variation of lived experience. My assertions will not align with those of every reader. However, it is important to explicate the ways in which linguistic and cultural practices historically associated with U.S. Whites have been empowered, whereas language and culture associated with non-Whites has been disempowered. More specifically, what has been called Black English, broken English, Black dialect, Ebonics, and/or Black speech has been disregarded and dismissed as anti-intellectual (Dandy, 1991; Smitherman, 2000; Warfield-Coppock, 1990). Although markers for White communication are viewed as acceptable within White societal structures, markers for Black communication are still seen as inconsistent and unacceptable within the same structures.

Throughout centuries of cultural miseducation and racial misrepresentation, Black communication practices have been positioned as picayune. These inequities create indelible tensions for Black communicators who feel a sense of double-consciousness and the need for communication strategies when interacting within predominantly White structures. For this reason, I interrogate the primary tensions that impact communication at micro and macrolevels.

THE ITERATIVITY OF RACISM

> Some things are just too unjust for words . . . and too ambiguous for either speech or ideas.
>
> —Ellison (1952)

Situating Black communication as intercultural communication requires an examination of its dialectical tensions. Racism contributes to a primary source of tension between and among U.S. communicators identifying as Black and White. Oppressive societal power is discussed repeatedly within the texts of Black American authors. Authors write to articulate and overcome the impact of racism. For example, in *Black Boy*, Richard Wright (1945) delineates the hegemonic power of color hate in the South where "the Black man grew in turn to hate in himself that which others hated in him" (p. 6). Elsewhere, Invisible Man attests that "African Americans constantly negotiate living in a White man's world" (Ellison, 1952, p. 289). Moreover, describing Southern racist ideology as threatening, hooks (1996) learns "to fear White folks without understanding what it is she fears" (p. 31). Likewise, in *Coming of Age in Mississippi*, Anne Moody (1970) gazes at the Jim Crow laws that hinder life for Blacks in the segregated South: "Our waitress walked past a couple times. . . . She asked us what we wanted. We began to read to her from our order slips. She told us that we would be served at the back counter, which was for Negroes. 'We would like to be served here,' I said" (p. 110). These and other observations contribute to a collective interrogation of oppressive societal structures. The talking drum is based in wholistic African-centered action to live, preserve, and foreground human well-being in every sphere of life. Our collective interactions are essential to overall freedom.

In *The Souls of Black Folk*, W. E. B. Du Bois (1903/1999) predicted, "The problem of the 20th century is the problem of the color-line—the relation of the darker to the lighter races of men in Asia and Africa, in America and the islands of the sea" (p. 17). Du Bois's words still ring true within 21st century structures. As a result, an active effort to expose, illustrate, and overcome racism is central to healthier communication practice.

The iterativity of racism—defined here as ongoing words and actions that work to describe and disassemble racism—is an overarching theme espoused by Black communicators. Racism is a symbolic and social construct with numerous rhetorical dimensions, and there is an increasing need to address racism within any communication practice. According to Asante (2003), African American rhetoric responds to racism in three primary ways: via discourse on correctives, efforts at reconciliation, and challenges to the last vestiges of White supremacy. Speakers and writers deal with one or more of these characteristics at any given time. Racism, White supremacy, White privilege, race subjugation, and Whiteness are perpetual factors within U.S. societal structures. Racism does not need to be obvious to be salient. To the contrary, racism is inferential and overt (Hall, 2003), cultural and systematic (McPhail, 1994; West, 1993), global and local (Cress Welsing, 1991), and personal and structural (Back and Solomos, 2000).

Fuller (1984) charged that racism works against non-White persons at any time or place, in one or more of nine interrelated areas of activity including economics, education, entertainment, labor, law, politics, religion, sex, and war. He argued "No other sociomaterial forces, by people, affect so many people, in so many places, so much, in so many areas of activity, as the factors of race and sex" (p. 23). It is important to note that racism moves beyond personal prejudice, to systemic oppression and systemic advantage.

Any exploration of the Black experience will ultimately include its contact with White racism. Consequently, the iterativity of racism functions to make racism visible. Fuller (1984) and Cress Welsing (1991) contend that understanding the power of racism begins with identifying its four stages:

1. Establishment of racism: Any individual thoughts, speech, and actions that help create a total pattern of racism
2. Maintenance of racism: Any speech and action that is continually practiced to directly or indirectly sustain racism and keep it a reality in one or more areas of activity
3. Expansion of racism: Any speech and action that directly or indirectly promotes and increases the number of people subjected to racism
4. Refinement of racism: Any speech and action working in a manner to improve methods of making racism more effective

Racism often becomes an ambiguous force which is rarely placed within a palpable definitive context. Erasing its strategic nature largely omits any responsibility for racism. Institutional racism and its machination impedes on intercultural and interracial communication. Scholars across disciplines seek to *overstand* the matrix of power in daily life (Asante, 1998, 2003; Cress Welsing, 1991; Fanon, 1967; Fuller, 1984; Houston & Davis, 2002; Gonzalez, Houston, & Chen, 2004; Kunjufu, 1986; Orbe & Harris, 2001; Staples, 1998) and call for more investigation:

> First, there is a need for greater theoretical clarity on key concepts. Second, there is a need to broaden the research agenda to cover issues that have been neglected, such as culture and identity. Third, there is a need to understand racism and how to counter it. Fourth, there is a need to integrate the analysis of racism with a conceptualization of related issues, such as gender and sexuality. (Back & Solomos, 2000, p. 23)

Machinations of racism occur through local discourse. Making racism visible means connecting its local applications with wider public discourse and developing sensitivity "to the trans-local matrices of racist culture and ethnic absolutist movements" (Back and Solomos, 2000, p. 24). To overstand racism is to act from the conscious awareness of the ways in which discursive and hierarchical social zones work to divide, fragment, and destroy human beings.

CONSCIOUSNESS

> Human beings are not born with automatic knowledge of who they are, what they have been and what they will become. This is taught by the society, through the family, the educational structures, the culture, the symbols and the religion of a people.
>
> —Akbar (1985, p. 26)

I am because we are. My consciousness is created in part through my interactions with other people. Various theories address the social, historical, and political forces that inform consciousness among communicators. According to Akbar, humans learn societal place via interactions with other humans. Elsewhere, Cooley's (1902) theory of the looking glass self suggests that self-awareness is mirrored on the eyes of other people. For example, have you ever attempted to change your appearance, attitude, or actions based on (what you believed to be) someone's perception of you? Did you alter your posture, eye contact, accent, language, or word choice because of (what you believed to be) another person's expectations? In many ways our societal positions are taught and assigned through our interaction with the world around us.

Human interactions are also influenced by our perceptions of reality. According to Berger and Luckmann (1967), consciousness is formed by the social construction of reality. Rather, human beliefs and behaviors are constructed through implicit and explicit societal rules. In some cases noncompliance with dominant rules will equate to social deviance. Therefore human interactions cannot be detached from society where social symbols, knowledge, and resources constitute a grand narrative. Through appropriation we as humans insert ourselves and others into that narrative (Gauntlett, 2002; Kellner, 2003). Communication is a vital part of that socialization process.

Black consciousness includes beliefs, perceptions, and issues of significance for Black Americans. This is the active mindfulness of self, life, and one's surroundings. According to Du Bois (1903/1999), Black consciousness includes particular tensions resulting from lived experiences. Like Karl Marx, Du Bois recognized that class, history, and society constrict human life. Beyond Marxist philosophy, Du Bois also recognized that racial distinctions and racial constructs are supremely important and central to how human beings experience the world. Du Bois believed that race and racism could not be extrapolated from questions concerning oppression. When addressing identity consciousness, Du Bois suggested that a metaphoric veil—or divide—exists between Black and White Americans. The veil symbolizes two Americas, where the Black self sees itself through the misperceptions of White society. The result is two dimensions of consciousness—described by Du Bois as double-consciousness: "It is a peculiar sensation, this double-consciousness, this sense of always looking at one's self through the eyes of others. . . . One ever feels this two-ness, two unreconciled strivings; two warring ideals in one dark body" (p. 3).

Demonstrating the degree to which Black identity is fragmented by numerous social restrictions resulting from imperialism, capitalism, and racism, Du Bois (1903/1999) writes: "Leaving, then, the world of the White man, I have stepped within the veil, raising it that you may view faintly its deeper recesses" (p. 5). By revealing and thus removing the veil, Du Bois exposes the terministic screen of Whiteness. The metaphoric veil represents Black America's perception of self as influenced by White America's perception of Blacks. The veil infiltrates almost everything having to do with the Black/African American experience.

Double-consciousness is a complex way of seeing and being seen. Arguably, Black communicators learn the rules of White culture in part by gazing through the veil. This erudition results in a particular epistemology known to Blacks, but about which Whites may be oblivious. Remaking consciousness is a strenuous and necessary process. Fanon (2000) argued that Blacks have been forced to exist within a civilization that has erased many of the customs and sources on which Black culture is based, and struggle within a civilization that has imposed itself upon them. This imposition works against Black consciousness. Any attempt to understand this complex ontology requires understanding a particular location: "Not only must the Black man be Black—he must be Black in relation to the White man" (Fanon, 2000, p. 257).

Consciousness also consists of history. James Baldwin (1971/1992) noted that people are trapped in history and history is trapped in people—an idea which serves as a point of departure for examining how history directly impacts our current cultural identities. African collective memory-perception competence—that is, critical memory—emphasizes a collective understanding of the pastness in the present (Gray, 2001). At its core, critical memory unveils the ways in which history matters in current and future contexts. Within this essay, *critical* refers to examinations of structural power and *memory* connotes the historical, social, and political experiences that impact our communication today. The next section further explores critical memory and communication strategy for Black communicators.

WAS WRIGHT WRONG? CRITICAL MEMORY AS SOCIOPOLITICAL CONTEXT

> In this great contest of right against wrong. . . . Who are the cowards, if not those who shrink from argumentation, the light of truth, the concussion of mind, and a fair field?
>
> —Sojourner Truth (1850/1998)

When Reverend Dr. Jeremiah Wright, Pastor Emeritus at Trinity United Church of Christ, addressed an audience of nearly 10,000 at a dinner sponsored by the Detroit Chapter of the National Association for the Advancement of Colored People (NAACP), he did so under a polarizing glare associating him with radical anti-Americanism. However, if the standards applied to Rev. Wright are measured against Dr. Martin Luther King Jr., then he too can be deemed a radical—along with Patrick Henry, The Dalai Lama, and anyone else who dares address societal ills. Some argued that Rev. Wright's reemergence occurred at the risk of staining the image of Barack Obama, the 2008 Democratic presidential nominee. Others characterized Wright's NAACP speech as redemptive success.

Building on the NAACP's theme, and a declaration made by the great soul singer Sam Cooke—*A change gon' come*—Rev. Wright challenged the dominant ideology and evoked a troubled but victorious

American past. Carved out of a continuum of Black liberation theology, his speech exemplified how Black communication became a unique form of critical intercultural communication. His analysis of power in language suggested that changing the world begins with words. For Rev. Wright, change is a concept best explored through the rhetorical lens. Drawing from African-centered rhetorical traditions—for example, humanizing and harmonizing, profound optimism, nommoic creativity and critical memory—Rev. Wright skillfully aligned, superimposed, and knotted together references to Black, White, Christian, Muslim, Jewish, and Native American groups for the purpose of foregrounding oppression in the 21st century.

Prior to the NAACP dinner, Rev. Wright's hyperbolic illustrations had been framed by the media as hate speech. Yet, his message remained the same: Racism continues to be one of the most influential and detrimental factors in everyday life. Rev. Wright made visible the multiple facets of intercultural and interracial experience that form the United States of America.

Language is the bloodline of culture and carries within it memories of the ways in which power remains in effect. Why did Rev. Wright infer race for persons cited in his speech? His approach recognizes how knowledge historically became legitimized in the United States. Thus, Wright strategically and repeatedly frames his research as informed by Black *and* White scholars for listeners who would not believe otherwise. Simultaneously the Black rhetorician unpacks palpable truths for those who understand that race almost always carries with it privilege and denied privilege.

Rev. Wright's strategy is nothing new. Throughout the American experience, Blackness has had a curious association with Whiteness. In some cases Whiteness legitimized Blackness. For example, in the 19th century, young Frederick Douglass (1845/1970) called on the credibility of Whites when learning to read and later for making a case against slavery. The Abolitionist and Suffrage movements overlapped for similar reasons: White woman could speak out against slavery when slaves could not do so without severe penalty. Moreover, at one time written passes sanctioned by Whites were used to grant slaves mobility between plantations. And today, I know from personal experience that educators use similar passes/strategies when exploring "controversial topics" that could be minimized and dismissed as coming from "the angry Black man."

To attenuate Rev. Wright's truths, one needs to examine the legacy on which the Black communicator builds his message. Rev. Wright is a former U.S. marine. As a cardiopulmonary technician at the National Naval Medical Center in Bethesda, Maryland, he was part of a 1966 medical team charged with caring for President Lyndon B. Johnson. Wright recalls having his credentials questioned by servicemen who did not believe that a Black man was capable of such responsibility. Wright's critical memory serves as a resource for deconstructing the ambiguous nature of racism. These theoretical perspectives speak to knowing and being in a racialized society where the experiences of marginalized groups fall below the radar of dominant culture:

> In the past, we were taught to see others who are different as being deficient. We established arbitrary norms and then determined that anybody not like us was abnormal. But a change is coming because we no longer see others who are different as being deficient. We just see them as different. Over the past 50 years, thanks to the scholarship of dozens of experts in many different disciplines, we have come to see just how skewed, prejudiced and dangerous our miseducation has been. . . . Ed Kennedy, today, those of you in the Congress, you know . . . Ed Kennedy today cannot pronounce cluster consonants. Very few people from Boston can. They pronounce park like it's p-o-c-k. Where did you "pock" the car? They pronounce f-o-r-t like it's f-o-u-g-h-t. We fought a good battle. And nobody says to a Kennedy you speak bad English. Only to a Black child was that said. (http://www.cnn. com/2008/POLITICS/04/28/wright.transcript)

Wright's comments reveal how the complexities of racism impact every sphere of social life. Something as simple, or complex, as language is often used to judge intellectual ability.

Carter G. Woodson (1933/1990) argued that to control a person's mind is to control that person's actions. Thomas Kochman (1981) called for a revolution over cultural and linguistic subordination. Andrew Hacker (1992) urged for the meeting of two nations, two realities, and two truths within America. By espousing the idea that "difference does not mean deficient," Rev. Wright acknowledges the ways in which race and culture are hierarchically situated in educational, organizational, and societal constructs. Indeed, within the United States, Black culture and communicators have been classified as deficient.

Geneva Smitherman (2000) found that cultural stereotypes hinder the communicative process for children. For example, a Black child might be called "deficient" for using the phrase "It be hot in here." Smitherman and others recognize the iterativity of *be* as perpetually and concurrently encompassing the past, present, and future. Thus for Black communicators "It be hot in here," might indicate that it was hot yesterday, it is hot today, and undoubtedly it will be hot tomorrow—three dimensions of time spoken in one simple word. Is this deficiency or rhetorical artifice? Perhaps it is time to *re-present* language and culture in North American school systems.

History lives on. Critical memories impact cultural identities and help to contextualize today's experiences. Every time we celebrate a birthday we are celebrating a sense of history. Black communication bridges the present to a past which has not yet dissipated. Racism continues to impact all potential freedoms. The critics would argue that Rev. Wright's comments endangered Sen. Obama's presidential hopes. But if the country were not ready for such a discussion, was it really ready for change? The race for the 2008 Democratic presidential nominee was laden with issues concerning race and gender. No doubt the media outlets understood the marketability of controversy, but something more was happening here. The world was being drawn to the synoptic stories of the *other* and sharing in the accounts of marginalized groups.

It is erroneous to assume that a common land or language justifies one culture. Reframing the sociopolitical contexts of communication requires an explication of power in its manifold layers. Only then can we begin to understand the process by which cultural bodies come into contact with one another. African-centered philosophy offers guidance on these complex issues. Rev. Wright did not claim to speak for and about all people. He used critical memory and communication strategy to implore one central idea: The less you think about oppression, the more your tolerance for it grows. We must consider whether Rev. Wright was really adhering to the way of *Maat*—thereby working to bring good into the world.

CRITICAL MEMORY AND THE QUEST TO BECOME THE FIRST BLACK U.S. PRESIDENT

Throughout his campaign to become the 2008 Democratic presidential nominee, Senator Barack Obama (D-IL) engaged critical memory. In "A More Perfect Union," Sen. Obama tapped into critical memory to reinforce his view on U.S. race relations and to strategically distance himself from Rev. Wright.

Wright had been accused of incendiary rants against White America. When the media began to question their 20-year friendship, Sen. Obama acted to save his race for the nomination. Responding with strategic communicative dissociation, Obama called on critical memory to distance himself from Wright and build on the ideology of change promised throughout his campaign:

> I am the son of a Black man from Kenya and a White woman from Kansas. I was raised with the help of a White grandfather who survived a Depression to serve in Patton's Army during World War II and a White grandmother who worked on a bomber assembly line at Fort Leavenworth while he was over-

seas. I've gone to some of the best schools in America and lived in one of the world's poorest nations. I am married to a Black American who carries within her the blood of slaves and slave owners—an inheritance we pass on to our two precious daughters. I have brothers, sisters, nieces, nephews, uncles and cousins, of every race and every hue, scattered across three continents, and for as long as I live, I will never forget that in no other country on Earth is my story even possible. (http://www.cnn.com/2008/POLITICS/03/18/obama.transcript/index.html)

In this example, memory captures the nature of consciousness. Sen. Obama illustrates how the stories we inherit work to shape us. In the process, he practices strategic distancing to avoid close associations with nondominant group members who challenge dominant ideology. Instead of aligning himself with Rev. Wright, Obama distinguishes himself as less threatening to dominant ideologies. He draws from the past to contextualize his current stance on race. His lived experience is positioned within a safer understanding of history.

It is interesting to observe how Sen. Obama claims an identifiable Black experience without suspending images of dominant American patriotism. His critical memory draws from the past to navigate today's social structures. This is a delicate negotiation indeed. At stake is the appearance of negating Rev. Wright's controversial statements and offending dominant group members. On the other hand, to satisfy other constituencies, Sen. Obama avoids minimizing the ramifications of the African Diaspora. Certainly too little or too much of either perspective can impact his standing among voters. At one point he compares Rev. Wright's words to those spoken by countless Americans, including the senator's own grandmother. Obama strategically sparks critical memory in the minds of his audience as a way to gain advantage and frame the situation:

I have already condemned, in unequivocal terms, the statements of Reverend Wright that have caused such controversy. For some, nagging questions remain. Did I know him to be an occasionally fierce critic of American domestic and foreign policy? Of course. Did I ever hear him make remarks that could be considered controversial while I sat in church? Yes. Did I strongly disagree with many of his political views? Absolutely—just as I'm sure many of you have heard remarks from your pastors, priests, or rabbis with which you strongly disagreed. (http://www.cnn.com/2008/POLITICS/03/18/obama.transcript/index.html)

Emphasizing a shared American experience allows Sen. Obama to gain the support of his largely White American audience. Yet he keeps Blacks involved in the discourse by acknowledging the past. He calls on his listeners to do the same. In the quest to become the first Black/African American U.S. president, Obama recognizes American history without creating barriers between himself and his diverse constituency. His strategy: racial tension is met with accommodation. By recognizing the past in the present, Sen. Obama constructs new alternatives for the future.

Black communication as intercultural communication rests in the complexities surrounding discourse between and among Black and White Americans. Inveterately, a dynamic montage of U.S. culture—including notions of history, privilege, and power—impact our perceptions. As Houston Baker (2001) notes, critical memory is concerned with how human beings are shaped by history, because a well documented past is a reliable guide for the future.

SUMMARY

Intercultural communication consists of the dynamic interplay between values, beliefs, norms, and practice. Black communication has been shaped in part by Black–White interaction. Myriad autobiographies, narratives, journal entries, and poetic stances explore this ever-changing phenomenon.

After considering the aforementioned ideas, one can argue that Black communication is a critical part of U.S. intercultural communication. Yet few studies focus on specific tensions and strategies particular to Black communicators. This book contributes to that discussion. It is not enough to know that difference exists. We must understand *how* it exists and *why* it matters. Racism impacts diverse groups in different ways. Consider the degree to which this notion is expressed in Delgado and Stefancic's (2001) report:

> Studies show that Blacks and Latinos who seek loans, apartments, or jobs, are much more apt than similarly qualified Whites to be rejected, often for vague and spurious reasons. The prison population is largely Black and Brown; chief executive officers, surgeons, and university presidents are almost all White. Poverty, however, has a Black or Brown face. People of color have shorter lives, receive worse medical care, [and] complete fewer years of school. (p. 10)

Subjugation works to the detriment of people everywhere. Marginalized group members know first-hand how oppression and privilege inform human interactions within organizations, institutions, and systems.

Undoubtedly, these ontological and epistemological experiences are prime issues for intercultural/interracial/cross-cultural communication research.

Certainly, time and healing have prompted societal progress. The ideas espoused in this chapter do not deny that progress. Still, after the historical election of its first Black/African American president, and after seating its first Hispanic American Supreme Court justice, the United States must continue to challenge its own oppressive practices. Far too many examples of Black–White interaction reverberate with inequalities, echo miseducation, and shriek inconceivably high unemployment, incarceration, and mortality rates. Beyond that are the faint whispers of prejudice, bias, and intolerance which leave little question that history permeates our current mind-state. The rhetoric of Wright, Obama, and others reveals the expression, resistance, and transformation of life in the United States and around the world. To understand Black communication is to better understand ourselves. The talking drum adds depth and clarity to that quest.

Two

AFRICAN-CENTEREDNESS, INTERCULTURAL COMMUNICATION, AND CRITICAL MEMORY

Africa has a gift to give the world that the world needs desperately, this reminder that we are more than the sum of our parts: the reminder that strict individualism is debilitating. The world is going to have to learn the funda- mental lesson that we are made for harmony, for interde- pendence. If we are ever truly to prosper, it will only be together.

—Desmond Tutu (2004)

This chapter consists of four parts. Part I describes the African-centered philosophy that drives this discussion. Part II discusses key theoretical paradigms for intercultural communication research. In Part III, I fore- ground critical-interpretative frameworks that speak to power, privilege and antiracist dialogue. In Part IV, I discuss critical memory and my own axiological position.

PART I: CONSTRUCTING
AFRICAN-CENTERED THEORY

African-centered theorizing envisions the world from the inside-out by placing the ontology, epistemology, and axiology of African descendants at the center of analytical discourse. The goal is to examine Black culture with descendants of Africa being the agents and actors of their own cultural-historical existence (Muhammad, 2000).

African-centered theorizing works to foreground Diasporic conditions often omitted from Western communication models, and locates Africa as a reasonable point of departure for raising academic inquiry. It is an ideology that positions descents of Africa as subjects rather than objects. The intent is never division or segmentation of humankind. Beyond cultural-nationalist expressions that foreground markers of oppression against Black people, proactive African-centeredness is concerned with making life better for all human beings (Karenga, 2003; Woodyard, 2003).

African-centered theorizing extends and refines elements of Afrocentrism and Afrocentricity. To some, Afrocentrism may connote ethnocentrism—which is the antithesis of Afrocentricity in general, and African-centeredness in particular. Afrocentrism, from a conservative view, may imply segmenting and separating Black people from the rest of America. Conversely, Afrocentricity illustrates a dynamic ideological perspective that bridges Africa to the rest of the world. Over the years, Cheikh Anta Diop, Molefi Asante, Maulana Karenga, and countless others have worked tirelessly toward an Afrocentric or African-centered perspective as an alternative worldview. In 1972, John Henrik Clarke described the project in this way:

> It is an international struggle on the part of people of African descent against racism and for a more honest look at their history. On university campuses and in international conferences, they are demanding that their history be looked at from a Black perspective or from an Afrocentric point of view. (Gray, 2001)

African-centered theory building speaks to underrepresented experiences and posits that the history of the nation or world cannot be interpreted exclusively from any one standpoint. This is a project that metaphorically relocates descendants of Africa in a social, political, philosophical, and economic sense for purposes of re-examining life and living.

African-centered theory has the potential to empower students of all cultures. It seeks to unite based on cultural agency and mutual respect for all people, by providing an ideological position and perception founded in aspects of African tradition. My African-centered framework is based in 13 key principles (Gray, 2001):

1. Humanizing and harmonizing: Humanity and harmony are essential to life. Life is a rhythm. Nature thrives on rhythm. Social interactions are based in rhythm where good bequeaths good. Humanizing and harmony do not necessarily equate to being a martyr because life's rhythm emphasizes living, and seeks to make valuable contributions to life.
2. Primacy of African people and civilization: This means to recognize the origin of the earliest known harmonious civilizations and argue for Kemet and Egyptian studies to be emphasized in all disciplines—particularly in communication and rhetorical studies which are strongly rooted in African traditions.
3. Prioritizing the African audience: This is to speak to various cultural audiences and emphasize a well-rounded education that foregrounds African experiences. Scholarly activity calls on the African American audience to refute miseducation about its culture.
4. Njia as theme: This is to practice profound optimism and ongoing voice/articulation of overcoming racism and oppression in both word and deed, including art, music, and poetry. Beyond mere survival, Njia is concerned with theorizing human achievement, writing, and educating for the purpose of freedom.
5. The way of Heru as theme: This is to make a conscious effort to resurrect and restore African descendants to a place of pride and confidence. Heru supports critical methods to produce confident, never doubtful, work—and maintains that cultural representation is essential to pride, unity, and self-empowerment.
6. Harmosis as mode: This is to synthesize ancient and traditional culture with contemporary culture (e.g., hip-hop culture, jazz). Harmosis intertwines the past and present and is founded in the work of writers, artists, and thinkers, because of whom African traditions live on.
7. Wholistic Afrocentric action as goal: This is to live, act, and educate to preserve and foreground human well-being in every sphere of life (e.g., oppressive thought + oppressive action = slavery). Action is essential for the possibility of freedom.
8. The Sankofan approach: This is to begin with history and recognize value in historical wisdom (e.g., Douglass, Washington, Du Bois, Garvey, etc.); to build on historic ideas and understand history as the foundation of the future.

9. Nommoic creativity: This is the power of the word. Words introduce new ideas and thoughts. Contemporary communication is fresh, innovative, and creative; and stretches for meanings not necessarily captured within established bounds of English language. Words lend to liberation and overall freedom.

10. Maatic argumentation: Truth, justice, and harmony work for the liberation and well-being of all human beings. We write, sing, build and model justice at all times. We work to articulate what life is currently, and can be.

11. Explicit locational indicators intentionality: This is to value ontological and epistemological explorations of the Black experience; and place Black ideas, characters, and thoughts at the center of relevant discussion. We do not rely solely on non-African ways to explicate African concepts and ideas (e.g., spiritual and cultural practice; language).

12. African collective memory-perception competence: Descendants of Africa are linked to a shared historical and experiential journey, and a shared memory base of feelings, attitudes, and proclivities resulting in a multidimensional nonmonolithic experience. Critical memory is the ability to touch, activate, and resonate with individuals and groups.

13. Nzuri as invitation and standard: This is to believe that beauty and goodness are synonymous and worth striving for in all efforts. Beauty is as beauty does, and contributes to good works.

These 13 principles reflect a rich intellectual tradition. Although freedom is an elusive sentiment, activist-intellectuals remain steadfast. When contemplating the definition of freedom, Assata Shakur articulates what freedom is not (Lynn, 2000). The Black communicator draws from experience to identify what freedom historically has not been, in order to recreate possibilities for what it can be. Similar to Shakur, I take agency and action in my research. I draw from African-centered principles as I work toward consciousness-raising. After all, what individual or group cannot benefit from consciousness-raising?

STRENGTHS AND CRITICISMS
OF AFRICAN-CENTERED FRAMEWORKS

Discourse reflects the substance of our culture. African-centered theory is a viable means to explore and explain the Black experience within America. Indeed, Black Americans have a unique cultural experience worthy of investigation. The rhetoric of resistance, transformation, and affirmation continues today. This experience, like other cultural phenomena, is not easily applicable to Western theories and methods.

Regarding criticisms of African-centered theorizing, some will argue that the African Diaspora is a thing of the past, and therefore warrants no special attention. Additionally, some suggest that African-centered thinking is potentially divisive. But scholars with a genuine interest in consciousness-raising understand that the consequences of the past live on today. The purpose of African-centered theory is not to divide or erase any cultural experience. Rather, it seeks to acknowledge particular views of the world. The major principles of African-centered theory cut across various intellectual positions: including Afrology—the study of African concepts, issues, and behaviors (Asante, 1998); Africology—a proactive stance that concentrates less on White racism and more on humanism (Woodyard, 2003); and Africanity—which refutes the subconscious separation of Africa from its descendants and includes all victims of the Diaspora, regardless of one's current global locations (Alkebulan, 2003). Consequently, African American rhetorical studies consist of and celebrate these many strands (McPhail, 2003).

African-centered theory does not separate Black and White Americans. To the contrary, this is an effort to interrogate unique cultural experiences bridging the continents (Gray, 2001). Moving beyond aesthetics, one does not have to dress in Kente cloth or celebrate Kwanzaa to engage in African-centeredness. These are not requirements but cultural celebrations of a rich African heritage.

Again, this theoretical perspective is not meant for divisive race/color based curriculums, but aims to appreciate culturally based approaches to education and multiple worldviews. African-centered thought is not founded in fantasy, false history, and false theory. It is founded in knowledge concerning cultural implications, traditional African components, cultural significant psychosocial cycles, and ideologies attributed to liberation (Warfield-Coppock, 1990).

African-centered thought informs many intellectual positions, including the following descriptions of Black masculinity theory, womanist thought, critical race theory, and theorizing the Black Atlantic.

BLACK MASCULINITY AND MANHOOD

Black masculinity and manhood explorations foreground the lived experiences of Black men across economic, educational, legal, and societal contexts (Jackson & Hopson, in press; Johnson & McCluskey, 1997; Staples, 1998); and call attention to the perceptual categories of fluctuating identities largely resulting from Western definitions of manhood

(Hecht, Jackson, & Ribeau, 2003). These explorations span from boyhood to manhood. By critiquing sociohistoric notions of race and gender, Black masculinity research emphasizes the ways in which daily practices of Black men are impacted by dominant structures (Odih, 2002).

BLACK FEMINIST
AND WOMANIST THOUGHT

Black feminist thought can be traced back to the words of enslaved women in the South and their contemporaries in the North (Houston & Davis, 2002). In response to a feminist agenda that largely negated the impact of race and culture, Black feminist theory prioritizes the lived experiences of Black women. This is the explication of Black women's unique perspectives for theoretic and practical purposes, and their intellectual and active resistance to subjugation (Hill Collins, 1990).

Womanist thought is a term popularized by Alice Walker (1983). The idea concerns the survival and wholeness of an entire people, female and male, as well as the valorization of women's works in all their varieties and multitudes. Womanist thought incorporates the multifaceted views of Black women who energize critical discourse necessary to rise out of race and gender domination (Awkward, 2000).

CRITICAL RACE THEORY

Critical race theory works to explain and transform systems based in race, racism, and oppressive power (Delgado & Stefancic, 2001). More specifically, critical race theory reveals the societal injustices that burden people of color, many of whom are disproportionately incarcerated, undereducated, underemployed, and disempowered. Recognizing that the United States has failed in many ways to condemn insidious and discreet policies, critical race theorists respond to unfair practices that do not take into account the complex linkages between race, class, and gender (Back & Solomos, 2000).

THEORIZING THE BLACK ATLANTIC

Theorizing the Black Atlantic recalls the transatlantic slave trade between Europe, Africa, and the Americas (Gilroy, 1993). This articulation of nationality acknowledges the multiplicity of Black experiences. Theorizing the Black Atlantic is a means and a method for exploring the connection between old and new worlds. By exploring race, culture, and power in European nations, the Black Atlantic emphasizes the Black experience beyond U.S. borders. Part II reviews literature relevant to critical intercultural communication research.

PART II: OVERVIEW
OF INTERCULTURAL COMMUNICATION

> Culture is the complete systemic co-ordinate way of life—the history, language, literature, poetry, drama, art, music, philosophy, religion, science, ideas, constructed through tools and objects— created by any group of people in struggle for survival and autonomy.
>
> —Toure (1963, p. 11)

Culture is a set of guidelines given and inherited by members of a particular group for how to view and experience the world, and relate to other people. Culture lends to the creation of identity, and is an amalgamation of the values, beliefs, and practices that distinguish us as individuals and groups. Culture informs our respective worldviews.

The process of intercultural communication occurs between worldviews and across racial, ethnic, and national boundaries (Kim, 2004). Academic explorations of intercultural communication date back to the 18th century (Potkay & Burr, 1995). But human existence has always included communication between and among different cultures. As a result of technology and globalization, intercultural communication has become increasingly prevalent, and operates today as a means for survival.

The term *intercultural communication* is credited to Edward T. Hall, whose focus on the intersection of culture and communication garnered attention in the 1950s. By examining the ways in which implicit cultural characteristics impact the process of communication, Hall developed a series of early intercultural communication models. These theoretical contributions continue to inform intercultural sensitivity frameworks today.

Intercultural communication holds multiple meanings, including the connection between diverse individuals and groups; assorted communication practices and styles; and discourse within multicultural communities. Additionally, Collier (2000) predicts that intercultural communication research of the 21st century will consist primarily of six categories: (1) naturally occurring talk of cultural groups; (2) increasing varieties of texts; (3) discourse as part of a local, global, social, and cultural context; (4) categories of cultural interpretation; (5) societal hierarchies; and (6) the function of meanings. When one considers the degree to which the world's population shares resources, today's communication research bears a great responsibility to recognize and address the markers of race, ethnicity, and culture that cut across each category. Misperceptions of speech, dress, and practice can muddle communication processes. Critical research includes attempts to understand and work through that muddle (Gudykunst & Kim, 1992).

ETHNOCENTRISM AND ETHNORELATIVISM

Bennett's (1993) developmental model of intercultural sensitivity lays out a continuum of social interactions. Ethnocentrism is a worldview limited by perceptions of one's own culture as right and other cultures as wrong. Cultural pride itself is not a problem. Being proud of one's culture lends to healthy self-esteem. But ethnocentric pride becomes problematic when attitudes negate, impede on, and endanger other individuals and groups. In the ethnocentric, or insensitive, stages one is opposed to cultural difference. Ethnocentricity assumes that one's own culture is all that is central to reality. According to Bennett (1993), ethnocentrism is based in intentional isolation and separation from others:

- Denial: Being unwilling to accept others; denying cultural difference (e.g., "I don't see us as different."); denying one's participation in dominant and oppressive power structures; denying the value of other cultures (e.g., speech, dress, customs, etc.)
- Defense: Defending oppressive power differences and societal positions ("Yes, we're different but it really doesn't matter."); defending one's right to contribute to and benefit from dominant worldviews; assuming a defensive stance against perceived difference
- Minimizing: Overlooking the effects of ethnocentricity (e.g., "You're one color, I'm another color, but we're all the same."); minimizing the value, concerns, and voices of other cultures; minimizing the need to transcend ethnocentrism

In the ethnocentric stages, dominant groups and systems choose to deny, defend against, and minimize the concerns of nondominant group members. When social and educational contexts dwell on the doings of the dominant group, the ethnocentric worldviews reinforce themselves and nondominant cultures and worldviews become virtually invisible. Both sides may internalize hegemony, particularly when dominant structures (e.g., academic institutions) make ethnocentrism a daily practice.

Conversely, Bennett's (1993) concept of ethnorelativism refers to stages of intercultural sensitivity. Here, one begins to recognize and accept multiple interpretations of the world; interactions with other cultures are predicated on grounds other than the ethnocentric protection of one's worldview; and one learns to work with difference rather than eliminate it:

- Acceptance: Crossing barriers of cultural difference and moving from isolation and separation towards intercultural sensitivity
- Adaptation: Adapting to new ways of thinking, without fear of losing one's own culture; cognitive frame shifting; learning to think outside of one's own cultural context
- Integration/constructive marginality: Taking on bicultural and co-cultural worldviews; transforming experiences and knowledge to become useful and valuable in any location; the constructive marginal is never "not at home" and oppression is never a fixed entity

Ethnorelativism recognizes identity challenges for nondominant group members, including the intercultural interactions that hinder personal development within dominant organizational, institutional, and societal structures (Landis, Bennett, & Bennett, 2004). These constraints impact communicators in different ways. Bouts with depression, isolation, anxiety, self-consciousness, and stress are just some of the reactions experienced by nondominant group members in oppressive social settings. Consequently, these emotional factors limit or eliminate possibilities for healthy communication.

The unique cultural location of the constructive marginal may create a catalyst for social change. The experiences gleaned from living on the margin of two cultures can help us learn from and eliminate tendencies to become overdependent on one source of identity. The experiences of marginalized group members are vital to increasing social consciousness. Intercultural communication consists of many unique experiences.

In terms of limitations, Bennett's (1993) model addresses the development of intercultural sensitivity without fully addressing the influence of power and racism. Therefore I extend Bennett's exploration to emphasize the impact of power on Black communicators. The underlying idea is that cultural growth and understanding requires advancing through stages of learning.

INTERCULTURAL COMMUNICATION PARADIGMS

Theoretical paradigms are methodological lenses to a particular set of scientific worldviews, ranging from empirical research to transcendentalism for social change. According to Martin & Nakayama (1999), a functionalist approach to intercultural communication research seeks to predict rather than describe human behavior. Here, culture is viewed as a variable, and empirical data focuses on cause and effect. A functionalist approach presumes objectivity. Science is seen as a series of arbitrary steps.

Next, an interpretive approach seeks to understand rather than predict. This includes hermeneutical and phenomenological research where themes emerge from the natural expressions of being human. Cultural interpretations are revealed through discourse, and explanations are not based solely on empirical evidence because the expression validates itself. Narratives, metaphors, stories, and myths take precedence over any presumed objectivity.

A critical humanist approach to research focuses specifically on the identification, rearticulation, and reformation of uneven power structures. Within this paradigm, culture becomes a site of struggle where meanings are contested and recreated. Essential to my exploration, critical humanism acknowledges power in language and calls for the productive transformation of that power.

Last, a critical structuralist paradigm advocates change from a deterministic standpoint, and focuses on the ways in which societal structures control and distribute resources. Here, the researcher emphasizes the ways in which society creates and maintains privilege. In this book, I move between interpretive, critical humanist, and critical structural paradigms, using what can be considered a critical-interpretive approach to research.

CO-CULTURAL COMMUNICATION THEORY

Co-cultural communication theory highlights the stories of people who struggle with unique circumstances. Moving between interpretive, critical humanist, and critical structuralist paradigms, co-cultural theory pushes the potential for co-existence without oppressive hierarchy. It is the essence of pluralism. Orbe's (1998) research reveals how societal power—ascribed, enacted, and adopted—informs communication among cultural groups. This power equates to dialectical tensions and strategies for nondominant communicators. Orbe (1998) explores some basic truths for co-cultural communicators. Co-cultural theory is based in five claims:

1. A societal hierarchy exists that privileges men, European Americans, heterosexuals, the able-bodied, and middle and upper social classes.
2. Dominant group members occupy positions of power that they use consciously or unconsciously to create and maintain systems that reflect, reinforce, and promote their experiences.
3. Dominant communication structures may impede the progress of those whose lived experiences are not reflected in public communication systems.
4. Nondominant group members share a societal position that renders them marginalized and under-represented within dominant structures.
5. Nondominant group members adopt certain communication behaviors when functioning within the confines of public communicative structures. (p. 12)

Co-cultural theory foregrounds specific tensions and strategies relating to intercultural and interracial communication. By arguing that race, gender, culture, sexual orientation, (dis)ability and social class matter during human interactions, Orbe's explication works to reveal the experiences, thoughts, and opinions of marginalized group members. The theory reflects a move towards meaning-making in lieu of empirical research which values objective examinations of nonrelational others. Thus, I use tenets of co-cultural theory to examine communication used to empower and disempower individuals and groups. Like oppression itself, co-cultural communication is complex in that its participants can be of the same ethnicity, orientation, sex, gender, and social class.

PART III: POWER AND PRIVILEGE

Part III concerns the societal power that impacts communication. Whether we realize it or not, power is always being negotiated during interactions. According to McIntosh (1988), racism evokes an inherent cultural privilege that puts White individuals and groups at an advantage and non-White individuals and groups at a disadvantage. As a White woman, McIntosh (1988) recalls unconsciously counting on unfair societal conditions not available to her Black co-workers. The author describes racism as an ambiguous and oppressive power that infiltrates thinking: "Whites are taught to view life as morally neutral, normative, average, and ideal, so that when we work to benefit others, this is seen as work which will allow them to be more like us" (p. 2). To further attenuate this idea, the following items are taken from a list of daily occurrences defined by McIntosh as characteristics of White privilege:

- I can arrange to be in the company of people of my own race most of the time.
- When I am told about our national heritage or about civilization, I am shown that people of my color made it what it is.
- I can be sure that my children will be given curricular materials that testify to the existence and the achievements of their race.

Essentially, this short list of privileges represents metaphorical spaces not necessarily accessible to non-Whites. The inability to relate to McIntosh's declarations may reflect a denied-privilege, stagnancy, or overall lack of personal freedom. Undoubtedly each experience must be interpreted on an individual basis. Through dialogue about privilege and denied-privilege we can begin to recognize the diversity in lived experiences.

There is always a possibility that notions of race and racism will impact Black–White communication. Marty's (1999) explication of antiracist dialogue makes palpable the ways in which communicators may encounter, resist, and work to eliminate rhetorical oppression. Like McIntosh, Marty calls for communicators identifying as White/European American to restructure and reinterpret the world from another vantage point. Marty (1999) offers the rhetorical steps, or stages, toward antiracism:

1. Self Reflection: To recognize the benefit and detriment of power and privilege
2. Re-envisioning the surrounding world: To include other cultures as lending to the world
3. Willingness to contribute to change: To recognize and accept the call to make a difference for the overall benefit of healthier intercultural interactions
4. Caring about intercultural relationships: To learn other cultural experiences; to listen
5. Reject racial privilege
6. Moving from admission of power and privilege to accountability: To take action toward intercultural sensitivity on a daily basis

Making antiracist dialogue part of daily practice may increase intercultural and interracial sensitivity. The value here is that Marty (1999) recognizes how passivity can inform and promote harmful ethnocentricity. To remain silent is to condone racism. Marty acknowledges that passivity can privilege and oppress individuals and groups, thus the author promotes active steps toward antiracism.

McIntosh (1988) and Marty (1999) position communication as part of a sociohistorical process. Their interrogations reveal societal power as witnessed by members of dominant groups. Similar to co-cultural communication theory and African-centered theorizing, McIntosh and Marty align with Martin and Nakayama's critical-interpretive-humanist paradigms. To various degrees, each perspective contributes to a particular understanding of Black–White communication.

PART IV: CRITICAL MEMORY
AS MEANS AND METHOD FOR DISCOVERY

> If history were the past, history wouldn't matter. History is the present, the present. You and I are history.
>
> —Baldwin and Meade (1971/1992)

> And even if you don't recognize my presence/ I am here.
>
> —Scott (2004)

In Part IV, I discuss critical memory as a means and method for discovery. Here, critical memory combines African-centered theory and Western qualitative approaches for the purpose of collecting and interpreting the shared experiences of co-cultural communicators.

Critical Memory as Means

Humans are shaped by history. The past dwells within us and, in many ways, informs who we are today. History, like culture, contributes to identity for many individuals and groups. Every time we celebrate a birthday, we are recalling and celebrating the pastness in the present. Critical memory is the art of rhetoric and remembrance. An African-centered principle, critical memory situates history as a viable intellectual resource where the past and present occur simultaneously. Its relevance increases over time. This is not a pretense to offer a full history, but to reintroduce salient topics for the sake of reflection and exploration. Building on rhetorical analyses, literary criticism, and phenomenology, critical memory explicates sensory knowledge through meaning gleaned from the written word.

The written word serves as a point of departure for rhetorical analysis. Words are powerful manifestations of the human capacity for symbolic behavior. Writers document and transmit cultural knowledge through words which then serve to bridge readers to past experiences. Words represent voices. African-centered theorizing avoids any rhetorical practice to control or omit these voices. Instead, traditions in African American rhetoric profess an art form that is expressive, purposeful, and spiritual by nature (Karenga, 2003; Woodyard, 2003).

Words are rhetorical symbols that structure meaning, common sense, and the reality of life. Critical memory focuses on the past to better understand society today. We are the culmination of our lived experiences. Documenting the past is one way to store our expanding realities.

Ideas about race, culture, and gender fill the critical memory. For example, Houston Baker (2001) remembers living in the segregated South where his father wore an "important-looking suit" in strategic attempt to gain respect, favor, and acceptance from a White dentist. Still, young Baker and his father are forced to wait until the office closes because the dentist refuses to serve Blacks during regular business hours. When the dentist finally agrees to see Baker, he neglects the young man's crooked teeth. Instead, as a remedy, the dentist tells Baker to contort his mouth:

> Then—as if some alien spirit imagined by Stephen Spielberg . . . his eyes rolled up. He began animatedly biting, scraping, and chewing at his upper lip, mumbling all the while: *"Can you see vat I'm doing? He can do it jus like zis?"* He had transformed before our eyes into a wildly distorted cubist portrait in the white light of the examining room. He kept mumbling through bites and scrapes of his teeth: *"Its kinda like monkeys, you know? Only zay exercise ze lower lip."* I could barely breathe. I wanted to get out of that dark green chair and escape this man's ideas about my mouth . . . about me . . . about my father. (p. 13)

Baker receives no real attention from the dentist, only instructions to contort his face like a monkey. Years later, Baker would recognize this humiliation as an ongoing tension during intercultural interactions. These memories fold into today. Baker's recollections spark in my own mind racialized experiences with a dentist, and a doctor, when I longed to flee for my safety. I remember how their comments about race and history had made me cringe, adding to a situation which was already painful enough. These were times when I, like Baker, laughed to keep from crying.

I journey back into the past to better understand the here and now. Through critical memory, I recognize yesterday's influence on my life.

My thoughts transcend boundaries of time and space as I recall incidents of oppressive power. Admittedly, I hold one understanding while Baker and others may hold something different. Still, our critical memories provide the means to foreground emergent issues of the day.

Critical Memory as Method for Discovery

My analysis is also based in Western approaches to research. In terms of qualitative method, my conceptualization of critical memory borrows from Stage (1999), Owen (1984), and McCracken (1988):

> First, one must become familiar with the context of the text. Second, a series of close readings are undertaken to identify and mark the vehicles employed by speaker(s). . . . The third step is to arrange the complete set of marked vehicles into subgroups by clustering those with similar entailments. . . . Fourth, a separate file of vehicles and their immediate contexts is compiled for each cluster of terms; that is one file for every concept. Finally the concept files are analyzed one by one for patterns within and between the cluster. (p. 73)

In the initial stages of my exploration, I read key texts without taking notes. Next, I reread the texts highlighting phrases, words, sections, and ideas associated with race, communication, and power. Third, I examined all highlighted portions and notations for repetition; recurrence; and forcefulness of ideas. According to Owen (1984), *repetition* refers to words and phases which repeatedly describe experiences and feelings; *recurrence* refers to consistent meaning expressed through different words; and *forcefulness* refers to the powerful ways that meaning is articulated (e.g., poignant verses and exclamations).

In the fourth step, I ordered preliminary themes and added written comments for purposes of reorganizing, reviewing, and synthesizing larger themes (McCracken, 1988). In the fifth step, I synthesized themes and their relationships to assess rhetorical invention, and to explore all representations with greater depth and clarity (Stage, 1999).

My insider-as-researcher position brings a culturally informed perspective to the critical-interpretive process. Drawing from my own critical memory, I recognize the polyphony of voices that add rich texture to the perceptions of Black communicators. Critical memory as a method is not complete at the thinking stage, but depends largely on conscious reflection and analysis of its recorded parts. Hence, one writes toward freedom. During critical-interpretation, only thick descriptions of interrelated parts will suffice. A thorough reflection on the documented parts is vital to understanding the whole of lived experience.

To understand a particular theme, it is necessary to consider the structure of its parts. Of course all lived experiences can be valuable sources of knowledge. But key slices of text lend to a better understanding of the whole. Sokolowski (2000) describes key slices as *pieces* and *moments* of lived experience:

> Wholes can be analyzed into two different kinds of parts: pieces and moments. Pieces are parts that can subsist and be presented apart from the whole; they can be detached from their wholes. Pieces can also be called independent parts. (p. 22)

Sokolowski (2000) compares the concept of pieces to acorns falling from a tree. After separation from the tree, acorns (pieces) continue to exist as independent entities. These pieces belong to the whole, yet they can become wholes in themselves. These pieces can be understood individually or in relation to the whole. In my examination the independent pieces include thoughts, phrases, and ideas that contribute to understanding Black communication as a whole.

Non-independent parts, called moments, cannot subsist or be presented apart from the whole. Moments are like colors that exist only when contrasted against other colors, or like time which gains significance only when measured against other periods of time. Moments cannot become a whole. However, moments are never minimized because a particular item can be a piece in one respect while being a moment in another.

Throughout my analysis, pieces and moments contribute to understanding intercultural interactions. In concluding this section, I offer my axiological perspective.

CONCLUDING THOUGHTS ON AXIOLOGY

> The practice of everyday life shapes and reshapes rhetorical acts, and puts forth and develops transforming and constantly transformed expressions.
>
> —Karenga (2003, p. 9)

My approach to intercultural communication research combines African-centered principles with Western rhetorical methods. Above all else, I want to contribute to efforts at bringing good to the global community. In the process of raising inquiry and naming specific communicative acts, I believe I can generalize without essentializing. In the spirit of consciousness-raising, deconstructing oppression takes precedence over accusation.

I seek to produce scholarship that meets the following criteria: (1) the work promotes multiple views of the world instead of one dominant worldview, and places the Black self inside that world; (2) the work suggests the realities of life are united in one grand manner; (3) the work moves from the material to the spiritual and accepts transcendental evidence; (4) and the work emphasizes cooperation, collective responsibility, cooperativeness, survival of the community, and nature.

Critical memory is a method and means for engaging the Black experience within intercultural and interracial contexts. In the next chapter, I employ critical memory to collect and interpret primary themes as a way to better understand critical intercultural communication.

Three

THE BLACK GAZE

This chapter begins my focus on primary themes as expressed by Black communicators. I begin with the iterativity of racism occurring across the rhetorical dimension of gaze. In the process, I discuss dialectical tensions associated with images of the Black-self as good–bad and visible–invisible; representations of terror; and how images are expressed, represented, and transformed during Black–White communication.

Undoubtedly, racism is a primary source of tension among Black communicators. Situating Black communication as a dynamic form of intercultural communication requires that we extrapolate the ways in which Black Americans negotiate this tension in voice, gaze, and space. Within most texts, societal power is discussed repeatedly. Efforts to expose, illustrate, and overcome racism suffuse Black literature. As such, my analysis focuses on the iterativity of racism—defined here as ongoing words and actions that work to describe and disassemble racism—and addresses its powerful impact on communication. A symbolic and social construct, racism has numerous rhetorical dimensions that deserve consideration if we are to comprehend and abolish the hierarchical zones that divide, fragment, and destroy human beings. In deconstructing the machination of racism, I begin by gazing at Whiteness.

GAZING AT WHITENESS

> Scholars, critics, and writers of color such as James Baldwin,
> Franz Fanon, Claude McKay, Zora Neal Hurston, Gwendolyn
> Brooks, Nikki Giovanni, Toni Morrison, bell hooks–have not only
> written about Whiteness, but their experiences of the ways in
> which Whiteness is socially constructed and functions as an
> oppressive, mythical norm that negates people, informs and fur-
> thers the need to understand and deconstruct it.
>
> —Martin and Davis (2001, p. 300)

To gaze is to see, stare, ponder, focus, envision, imagine, and/or examine power within social relationships. It is to challenge oppressive power
by exposing it. For example, North American slaves were forbidden to
look into the eyes of slave owners and overseers, as a way to maintain
the power structure. Looking dominant power in the eye was punishable
by violence or worse. One might argue that fear resulting from this historical practice continues today for Blacks hesitant to identify and confront oppression in predominantly White societal structures.

Gazing at Whiteness also refers to visual and imagistical representations of race, power, and privilege. This includes critical observations
associated with White/European Americans. Within the United States
and around the world, societal groups represent and are represented by
societal frameworks. As such, gazing at Whiteness involves exposing
societal power by describing its rhetorical characteristics.

According to Dyer (1997), "White people are systematically privileged in Western society and enjoy unearned advantage and conferred
dominance" (p. 9). As noted by Frankenburg (2000), Whiteness is a
structural advantage and race privilege often associated with White
America. Ralph Ellison's (1952) *Invisible Man* described Whiteness as
"White folks, authority, the gods, fate, circumstances, the force that
pulls your strings until you refuse to be pulled anymore. The big man
who is never there" (p. 118). A socially constructed phenomenon,
Whiteness is not easily identified and has historically occupied a position of just being human as opposed to occupying an assigned position
of race, where non-Whites become something other than human (Dyer,
2000). Consequently, race is often mistakenly colored everything except
White, to the extent that Whiteness becomes virtually invisible. For
young Richard Wright (1945), gazing at Whiteness is one way to make
it visible:

> It was in this manner that I first stumbled upon the relationships
> between Whites and Blacks, and what I learned frightened me.
> Though I had long known there were people called White peo-

ple, it had never meant anything to me emotionally. I had seen White men and women upon the streets a thousand times, but they never looked particularly white. To me they were merely people . . . yet somehow strangely different. (p. 30)

Gazing at Whiteness includes the ongoing observation and articulation of power that creates, enacts, and maintains White as exclusive to all that is normal and good in society. The Black gaze penetrates racialized constructions of life. Wright's observation of segregated Memphis exemplifies critical observations of co-cultural groups in general and Black Americans in particular. Conceptualizing Whiteness emphasizes a shared and multidimensional experience of oppression. Questions about Whiteness begin at an early age. Wright's need to understand race is both physiological and psychological. It is a hunger to understand his place in the world.

Conversely, the White gaze seals the Black child into crushing objecthood. Before facing more severe realities, he is forced to contemplate the inner workings of a racialized society. At age 6, Wright ponders the creation and origins of Whiteness that exist "somewhere in the background of the city as a whole" (p. 31). He knows that White people exist but he does not understand the power of the color-line. Like other Black children, Wright's young mind grapples with the social construction of Whiteness: "Whenever I saw White people now I stared at them, wondering what they were really like" (p. 31).

Gazing at Whiteness occurs when Wright's mother relocates her two children from one Southern city to another. During their travels, young Wright observes ticket windows and train cars separated by the color-line. Curious about this distinction between Black and White, he asks if he can "go peep at the White folks". This is a phenomenon worthy of scrutiny. The Black gaze also contemplates ways in which race, power, and privilege apply to his light-skinned grandmother. Wright knows the elderly woman is like him in many ways but, for all visual purposes, his Granny looks White. He wonders how Granny's light skin measures up against other White skin. Wright inquires, "Moma, is Granny White?" His mother offers little more than tepid answers. The child remains inquisitive. "I mean do White folks think she's White?" He presses the issue: "Granny looks White. . . . Then why is she living with us colored folks?"

How one becomes White is a pivotal theme here. The Black gaze is concerned with identity and asks how one gains power and privilege. Rather, how does one become White? Wright knows there are societal advantages. Yet gazing at Whiteness goes beyond skin color. Wright continues to question the sociopolitical implications of race, "Did Granny become colored when she married Grandpa?" Finally, "Why didn't Granny marry a White man?" (p. 56).

Simple questions are sometimes the most difficult to answer. *Can one become White?* Throughout slavery and beyond, some Blacks passed for White (meaning they represented themselves as White citizens) as a way to access mobility. Today Whiteness refers largely to societal power characterized by few physical markers (Dyer, 1997). It is erroneous to suggest that all White skin is privileged in the same way, just as it is naïve to neglect the societal benefits that result from close associations with Whiteness. Wright's interrogation reflects life in a society that devalues people of color. His treatment of race symbolizes the Black child's perception of self as connected to and disconnected from the surrounding world. Clearly, perceptions of skin color feed into a system of social and psychological restrictions that encourage or discourage societal participation.

The United States continues to be a society where children learn to associate value with White skin, hair texture, body type, and overall physical appearance. By and large, images of Whiteness have been associated with beauty, pride, and freedom. Without proper encouragement, Black childhood is impacted by perceptions of Whiteness that it can never become.

Remembering Whiteness

Last Friday afternoon
While we waited in the credit union drive-thru
My five year old daughter declared, "I wish I was White"

I was delayed by memories
Of my son saying the same thing
Although his grade school teacher had claimed
a multicultural attitude
Perhaps she was more harmful to my son

Now my daughter commenced to change her story
When asked why she began to deny
Even though we heard her plain as day

Her conversation is telling
And took me back to a time
When I too wanted to be White
Because they got all the best stuff

But I remember my father's words,
"Don't let me hear you say that again."
He taught me about pride, beauty, history, and racism
So that I might teach my own children

—Hopson (2005)

When my daughter became concerned about being the only Black person in her kindergarten class, she began to ask critical questions. Like young Richard Wright, she was curious as to how one becomes Black or White, and more specifically whether these categories are assigned or inherited. She had a vague idea that the answers to her questions were concealed within the attitudes and convictions of the world around her. Indeed, critical memory suggests that (mis)perceptions of race and power are increasingly important to the Black child's identity.

My own earliest memories of race include a time I was turned away from a birthday party because the birthday girl's parents refused to have a Black child in their home. I was 5 or 6 years old and lived in a predominantly White suburb in West Michigan. I had walked to the party with my neighbor, Tracy, who was White. Upon our arrival, the birthday girl and her mother stopped us at the front door.

Almost 30 years prior to my situation, Wright (1945) encountered a similar experience. Arriving at an event sponsored by the Communist Party, Wright reported "During the trip I had not thought of myself as a Negro. . . . Now I stood watching one White comrade talk frantically to another about the color of my skin, I felt disgusted" (p. 95). Like Wright, this had been my situation. I also stood silent, watching Whites engaged in discussion about me. At the conclusion of their whispering, I was told I could not enter the party. They quickly disappeared with no further explanation.

I remained outside for a while, perhaps trying to figure out what had just happened. Maybe I had hopes that they would reconsider. Instead I was told to move away from the porch. I walked to the curb confused and maybe a little embarrassed. Later Tracy told me, I had not been allowed inside because I was Black. At that point I wanted to become White, at least for a little while.

The birthday party was not an isolated encounter for me. I was one of a few Black children in a school where I was constantly reminded of that fact. Teachers and students did not celebrate me in the same ways they celebrated Whiteness. Their words, actions, and attitudes, however unintentional, constructed Whiteness as likeable, lovable, intelligent, and normal. It was obvious to my young eyes that I was the outsider-within. In my desire for favor, I observed Whiteness closely and familiarized myself with its speech and actions. Sometimes I tried to emulate Whiteness for the purpose of blending in and gaining mobility. Like Wright (1945), "I was learning how to watch White people, to observe their every move, every fleeting expression, how to interpret what was said and what was left unsaid" (p. 200). For the Black communicator, the gaze informs various intercultural communication strategies.

BLACKNESS AS VISIBLE-INVISIBLE

You're hidden right out in the open—that is, you would be if only you realized it.

—Ellison (1952, p. 118)

I remember trying to blend in with Whiteness hoping to resist the labeling, profiling, and stereotyping often experienced by Black communicators in predominantly White structures. Thus began my own sense of double-consciousness. Within dominant structures, I learned the unspoken rule—the closer to Whiteness, the better. Throughout maturation, I attempted to resist and transform this racialized power. I tried to curtail the unspoken rule using refined communication strategies.

As a teen I learned that young Black men are often profiled against racist stereotypes held by law enforcement. For example, in my attempt to avoid "DWB" (a theory that espouses the risks of *driving while Black*) I tried to hide out in the open. I worked to look less like the mediated stereotypes of Black men. Sometimes I removed my cap when driving through predominantly White areas of town. At other times I avoided areas with a heavy police presence. Although my strategy might seem questionable, Du Bois's (1903/1999) metaphoric color-line was very real to me. I oscillated between visibility and invisibility. Even when I sought to be visible for moral and political reasons, I also tried to become invisible for self-protection.

Critical memory reveals a common visible–invisible dialectic for the Black communicator. Invisible Man feels the tension whenever the inner eye of Whiteness refuses to acknowledge the Black body, which is left unseen by the "peculiar disposition of the eyes of those with whom I come into contact" (Ellison, 1952, p. 3). At other times, his safety and welfare totally depend on the ability to remain unseen and inconspicuous within White society.

For me, the tension becomes strategy when the Black body fades into the dense background of Whiteness, and I (possibly) avoid racial profiling. At other times, the tension arises "When they approach me [and] see only my surroundings, themselves, or figments of their imagination" (Ellison, 1952, p. 3). Back and forth, being invisible may be useful and advantageous if it sustains one's well-being and mobility. But, as Ellison contended, being invisible can perpetuate doubt of one's own existence and lead to a painful condition: "You ache with the need to convince yourself that you do exist in the real world" (p. 3). This adjustment is both a conscious and subconscious act that gets more complicated by the minute—to the point the process becomes constraining. Most certainly, the Black body informs one's experience in the world.

Black consciousness absorbs the lessons taught by White society. Like Ellison (1952) and Wright (1945), Blacks learn to watch, interpret, and read meanings and motives of Whites. These efforts constitute a communication strategy meant to decrease suspicion and obstruction, and increase mobility and acceptance. To be Black in America is to occupy grossly different spaces. Reinterpreting the world entails looking at one's self through the eyes of the oppressor, and simultaneously figuring that reflection into one's perception of reality. This duality highlights an oscillation between two souls, two thoughts, and two warring ideals of Black existence. Double-consciousness includes gazing at oppression; gaining an awareness that directly refutes grand narratives dedicated solely to White/European American progress; and seeking emancipation from the effects of slavery.

"Whiteness, stated or unstated, in any of its various forms leaves one invoking the historically constituted and systematically exercised power relations" (Nakayama & Krizek, 1999, p. 102). This is the power of the unspoken rule. At times, the Black intersubjectivity is mediated even when the White other is absent (Gibson, 2003). When social and educational contexts dwell largely on the doings of the dominant group, the result includes ethnocentric worldviews that reinforce themselves over time and become virtually invisible.

Black communicators within predominantly White structures experience fluctuating levels of acceptance and rejection. Communication is essential to identity development. To be labeled as wrong is to be identified as such. This is why Smitherman (2000) warned against a total reliance on European language and culture that facilitates an increasing rupture from Blackness.

When it comes to language and identity, all sides of the dominant worldview have internalized hegemonic oppression. For example, removing my cap to avoid racial profiling may have contributed to my own oppression. The dominant structure makes ethnocentrism a daily practice in education, employment, law, and health. Within each of these areas, Whiteness is the primary measure of correctiveness. As such the Black communicator asks the question, "Who am I in relation to others?"

> Human beings are not born with automatic knowledge of who they are, what they have been and what they will become. This is taught by the society, through the family, the educational structures, the culture, the symbols and the religion of a people.
>
> —Akbar (1985, p. 26)

The aforementioned quote applies to my own experience. Like young Richard Wright, I did not fully understand the extent to which dominant institutions marginalize children whose identities do not mesh with the grand narratives of predominantly White societal structures. Nor did I understand how this socializing occurs through myths and folklore. Like my daughter, I faced the unspoken rule: In this society the closer one is to Whiteness, the better.

Cultural privilege plays out at every level of society. For example, the Scholastic Aptitude/Reasoning Test (SAT) is believed to predict academic and intellectual potential for college students. Yet, some scholars have argued that such tests work more to discern knowledge about mainstream White culture. In 2005, Yale University psychologist Robert Sternberg argued to replace the SAT with the "Rainbow Project," a test which emphasizes creativity and open-ended problem-solving skills largely overlooked by the SAT.

Children learn skills necessary for success in their respective cultures. Whether the alternative aptitude tests will be accepted on a national scale is yet to be seen, but Sternberg's efforts speak to the ways in which language and lived experiences impact learning and development. Other efforts also take culture into consideration, including the Appalachian Intelligence Test (AIT) which addresses testing methods in lower economic and rural geographic regions; and Ruby Payne's (2001) framework for understanding poverty and its impact on the learning process.

In 1972, Robert Williams's Black Intelligence Test of Cultural Homogeneity (BITCH) reconstituted language as a way to expose cultural bias. Williams's test illustrates distinctive and dynamic truth. The short sample below tests the reader's cultural knowledge:

1. *CPT* means a standard of
    (a) time?
    (b) tune?
    (c) tale?
    (d) twist?

2. *Main Squeeze* means?
    (a) to prepare for battle?
    (b) a favorite toy?
    (c) a best girl/boyfriend?
    (d) to hold up someone?

3. *Nose Opened* means?
    (a) flirting?
    (b) teed off?
    (c) deeply in love?
    (d) very angry?

4. *Playing the Dozens* means?
   (a) playing the numbers?
   (b) playing baseball?
   (c) insulting a person's parents?
   (d) playing with women?

5. *Shucking* means?
   (a) talking?
   (b) thinking?
   (c) train of thought?
   (d) wasting time?

The BITCH test illustrates the critical juncture of language, culture, and content. Varying degrees of truth are reflected in the sample questions. Even with the generational gap, I'm sure some communicators can relate, whereas others may be further removed from these cultural expressions. Linguistic expression is quite *uncommon* and may indicate that universal and completely unbiased tests are nearly impossible. Nondominant group members face these dominant assumptions at almost every societal level. (Answers: 1 = a, 2 = c, 3 = c, 4 = c, 5 = d)

Children and adults are socialized into accepting the value system, history, and culture of European Americans. For example, in *Bone Black,* bell hooks (1996) explores how Blackness has been situated to represent inferiority when measured against the popularized images of Whiteness. Growing up in the South, hooks notices that the term *good hair* implies favorable hair that is "straight, not kinky, [that] does not feel like balls of steel wool" (p. 91). Conversely, *nappy hair* means bad hair and is considered a derogatory term used to minimize Black hair and by extension Black people. Throughout childhood, hooks notes the ways that hair symbolizes acceptance or rejection. The unspoken rule is that hair and skin tone are politicized as good or bad. As a Black child, hooks gazes upon a dominant culture that minimizes Black hair and Black girlhood. Her identity is impacted by these societal messages. Consequently, hooks and other scholars call for research documenting prejudicial experiences in all their variations.

Thinking back to the birthday party, I recall how being refused entry influenced my ideas about identity. That evening, in the presence of my father, I bluntly declared, "Daddy, I wish I were White." It would take almost three decades and children of my own for me to understand the enormity of patience and control in my father's response. "Why do you say that?" he asked. "Because they get all the best stuff," I answered. Undoubtedly, the gist of my reasoning was based on my own notion of good. I remember my father taking his time to formulate a thoughtful response. As the result of his teaching, my insecurities were transformed into Black consciousness.

Later, when my own children attend a predominantly White elementary school, I see similarities in our respective experiences. Their faces transport me back to my formative years, and I pray they do not feel the rejection I felt at that young age. There are years when I do not see any faculty of color. The fact becomes more apparent in the class photos that hang in the school's hallways. Spanning the last twenty years, I see few children of Asian and Indian descent, fewer Black children, and an all-White teaching staff.

Gazing into the old photos, I wonder how these children manage the intercultural tensions that I grew to know all too well. Have any made the same wish I made as a child? Obviously, my daughter did. What about the young men? Have any been pulled out of class like my son, and accused of vandalizing a desk? In a profane attempt to prove my son culpable, the teacher went into his desk, took out his scissors, and cut into the wood—*"Here you did it just like this didn't you?!"*

Fortunately, children are blessed with resilience, and maybe parents bear the brunt of critical thinking. As a child, hooks (1996) did not fully understand how poverty and racism impact people in her community, or why Black children are bused to a small country school: "As they are riding the school buses they pass school after school where children who are White can attend without being bused, without getting up at the wee hours . . ." (p. 5). Her father argues that the long walk benefits the children, and adds tales of walking miles to school through fields without boots or gloves. Perhaps this is his attempt to rationalize oppression. Perhaps this is a father's attempt to make oppression bearable.

Sometimes during interactions with teachers and administrators, my concerns are met with cynicism and contempt. I feel I am framed as the overly sensitive Black man, one who is consumed with race. This is the price I pay for consciousness. I fear for my children and worry that insidious self-inferiority will result from the ethnocentric educational processes that go unchecked. Also, I worry that my children will become unconscious and indifferent to oppression. As Akbar (1985) argued, at best Black children in racist societal structures can only hope to become objects of White culture, never its subjects. To embrace a self-defeating ideology is to hope for pseudo recognition by dominant society, that is, a White mask.

At the same time, I have multiracial and multicultural allies who give me hope. Many of them have their own obstacles to contend with, and we provide each other with support. Still, I wonder whether I am like hooks's father, rationalizing oppression by telling myself these real world experiences will help my children learn to succeed at an early age. That's when my critical consciousness argues back: *When teachers show little interest in working successfully with Black children, then Black children will suffer in school.*

Black communication and intercultural communication consist of contradiction and ambivalence. The intellectual resources of Wright (1945), Ellison (1952), and hooks (1996) are a valuable foundation for observations like mine. The Black gaze is necessary for exploring how race is played out interactionally: "Just as the eye is not simply a mirror, but a correcting mirror, the racial gaze is not a human condition but a social construction that can be resolved by correcting cultural errors" (Gibson, 2003, p. 31). If one is not careful, racism can suspend and even negate reciprocity. Correction is accomplished in part by turning to critical memory. The next section explicates representations of terror, rhetorical and otherwise, within the Black imagination.

WHITENESS AND REPRESENTATIONS OF TERROR AND ABUSE

> As long as I live and I can do anything about it, niggers are gonna stay in their place. Niggers ain't gonna vote where I live. If they did, they'd control the government. They ain't gonna go to school with my kids. And if a nigger even gets close to mentioning a White woman, he's tired o' livin'. I'm likely to kill him. . . . I'm going to make an example of you just so everybody can know how me and my folks stand.—Bryant (as quoted in Metress, 2002, p. 207)

The Black gaze falls upon themes of terror and abuse. Critical memory underscores the evasive but constitutive power relationships often omitted from discussions about intercultural communication. Referring to a historical period of racial apartheid and legal segregation, hooks (1992) describes "terror as a representation of Whiteness in the Black imagination" (p. 174). Interestingly, hooks foregrounds terror in ways similar to Wright (1945) and Ellison (1952). Their collective texts reveal that intercultural communication can be a complicated and traumatic endeavor for Blacks. For example, critical memories of girlhood depict a racialized climate where hooks (1996) "learned to fear White folks without understanding what it is she fears" (p. 31). Consequently, the author calls for expanded observations of racialized terror.

Black communicators describe intercultural interactions marked by abusive power. Some narratives depict graphic examples of physical and rhetorical terror to the extent that Blacks are taught to fear Whiteness. Hostility directed against Blacks is such a common occurrence in the 20th century American South that White men seem to possess a unique authority (Ellison, 1952). Lynching was a threat "which hung over every Black male in the South" (Wright, 1945, p. 190). For the Black communicator, every interaction with Whiteness includes the potential for bodily harm. The threat of aggression, real or imagined, wields tremendous hegemonic power.

While working at a clothing store, Wright witnesses a rape. As the storeowner and his son drag the Black woman into the store, people pass by with little more than a second look. A police officer observes but says nothing. Wright hears screams coming from the back room of the store. Later he watches the woman stagger out, clothes torn, bleeding and crying. The police officer accuses the woman of being drunk and takes her away in a patrol wagon. When Wright (1945) enters the store, he is told, "Boy, that's what we do to niggers when they don't pay their bills" (p. 199). The storeowner extends a cigarette and Wright is forced into a gesture of acceptance.

Wright is gripped by fear and powerlessness. The officer's silence condones the violence. The storeowner has been given a social pass. Confronting the perpetrator means risking one's livelihood. But risking life and limb for justice is not outside the realm of possibility. Dialectical tensions surface in trying to balance personal safety against the moral imperative of justice. Wright described the sense of powerlessness, "After they had gone I sat on the edge of a packing box and stared at the bloody floor until the cigarette went out" (p. 199).

Heading home, Wright continues to experience terror. After puncturing a bicycle tire, he accepts a ride from White men. As he steadies himself on the car's running board, he is smashed between the eyes with an empty whiskey bottle:

> "Nigger, ain't you learned no better sense'n that yet?" asked the man who hit me. "Ain't you learned to say sir to a White man yet?" Dazed I pulled to my feet. My elbows and legs were bleeding. Fists doubled, the White man advanced, kicking the bicycle out the way. "Aw, leave the bastard alone. He's got enough," said one. They stood looking at me. I rubbed my shins, trying to stop the flow of blood. No doubt they felt a contemptuous pity, for one asked: "You wanna ride now, nigger? You reckon you know enough to ride now?" (Wright, 1945, p. 200)

Bleeding, Wright jumps off the car. There is no assurance for his safety and fighting back could get him killed. Historically, the law often represented anything but protection. The Black communicator is forced to endure threats of violence.

Wright also described terror as entertainment for Southern Whites. For example, as the result of a wager between his co-workers, Wright is forced to fight Harrison, another Black man. Initially, Wright and Harrison refuse to fight. Later they agree to fight in order to earn 5 dollars each and to avoid violent retaliation. After submitting to the power and control of his co-workers, Wright explains, "I suppose it's fun for White men to see niggers fight. To White men we're like dogs or cocks" (p. 260).

Wright's comment speaks to a historic practice of terror as entertainment. During American slavery some Blacks were forced to participate in "nigger fights" where slave owners from nearby plantations gathered together their best fighters for battle (Howell, 2004a). These fights were quite popular and it was not uncommon for Whites in attendance to lay wagers on a potential winner.

A similar situation occurs when Invisible Man (Ellison, 1952) is invited to deliver his graduation speech to the town's leading White citizens. Upon his arrival, Invisible Man is forced into the battle royal where young Black men are placed in a makeshift boxing ring and made to fight each other. The audience consists of bankers, lawyers, judges, doctors, fire chiefs, teachers, merchants, and a pastor—all of whom represent the power of Whiteness. When the superintendent of schools introduces "the little shines" Invisible Man learns that abuse takes multiple forms.

> We were rushed up to the front of the ballroom, where it smelled even more strongly of tobacco and whiskey. Then we were pushed into place. I almost wet my pants. A sea of faces, some hostile, some amused, ringed around us, and in the center, facing us, stood a magnificent blonde—stark naked. There was dead silence. I felt a blast of cold air chill me. I tried to back away, but they were behind me and around me. Some of the boys stood with lowered heads, trembling. I felt a wave of irrational guilt and fear. (Ellison, 1952, p. 16)

The young Black men are aware of the consequences for gazing at a White woman. Historically, the act has been punishable by death. When the townsmen begin to grope the naked woman, Invisible Man reports, "I saw the terror and disgust in her eyes, almost like my own terror and that which I saw in some of the other boys" (Ellison, 1952, p. 17).

Blindfolded and girdled in cigar smoke and the stench of alcohol, the young men hear taunting from the onlookers: "Let me at that big nigger!" . . . "Let me at those black sonsabitches!" . . . "I want to get at that ginger colored nigger. Tear him limb from limb!" Ironically, Invisible Man oscillates between giving in "to a sudden fit of a blind terror" (p. 17) and searching for comfort in the familiarity of the superintendent's voice. Throughout the evening, Invisible Man receives blow after blow. Yet, he continues to think about his speech. Focusing intently on the future is his strategic attempt to endure the pain of the pres-

ent. The narratives of Ellison, Wright, and hooks are replete with examples of violence. "This was the culture from which I sprang. This was the
terror from which I fled" (Wright, 1945, p. 281).

Communicators have long explored representations of terror in the
Black imagination. In 1955, Emmett Till was beaten to death by men
who accused him of whistling at a White woman. This terror became
concretized in the Black imagination. Poems by Langston Hughes and
Gwendolyn Brooks immortalize the lynching of Till. Billie Holiday's
"Strange Fruit" and Nina Simone's "Mississippi Goddamn" express the
rampant lynching of Black men in the 20th century.

In "4 Little Girls," Lee & Pollard (1997) document the rhetoric of terror surrounding the 1963 Birmingham, Alabama church bombing that
killed four Black girls. At the time of the bombing, more than one-third
of Birmingham's police force was thought to be affiliated with the Ku
Klux Klan (Nunnelly, 1991). Birmingham's commissioner of public safety, T. Eugene "Bull" Connor led the police department, fire department,
board of education, public library system, and other municipal areas. In
addition, Connor was the embodiment of racist terror and the quintes-
sential segregationist. His authority and influence spanned the region,
and his dictatorial regime left little room for justice as it related to
Birmingham's Black population. Former mayor of Atlanta, and U.S.
ambassador, Andrew Young recalled Connor's power: "There was
almost no way to talk to him or reason with him. It was his town. It was
almost like the old West, where he was one-man rule" (Lee & Pollard,
1997). Eskew (1997) describes Conner as epitomizing the anxieties of
the White lower middle class. Reverend James Bevel remembers Connor
as a violent threat to Black life:

> When he saw any strength or self-respect in a Black person he
> just went crazy. He couldn't stand it. It's like, when you see me
> you gotta squat. So, if you don't become ingratiating he'd just go
> crazy. (Lee & Pollard, 1997)

Intimidation tactics were often used against Blacks in the segregated
South. Vicious dogs, fire hoses, and army tanks were used to construct
and maintain a racist order. Birmingham was so notorious for its terror-
ist acts that it was also known as "Bombingham." In Lee's documentary,
we are presented with black and white footage of a large tank moving
through the city streets. The image resembles a war-torn country,
except for the background containing familiar scenes of American made
automobiles and corner stores. Accompanying the footage, a voice
recalls Bull Connor as the representation of terror in the Black imagination: "He had a white tank that he would ride through the Black neighborhoods and terrorize people." Destruction was not uncommon. The

potential for danger lurked around every corner. And then there was the 1963 Sixteenth Street Baptist Church bombing.

> *As the children prepare for Sunday morning church service—playing laughing, talking, living—they are met with an unexpected attack on humanity. Moments before the explosion, the church phone rings. A child answers only to hear an unidentified voice on the other end.*
>
> *"Three minutes."*

Denise McNair dies at age 11. Carol Robertson dies at age 14. Addie Mae Collins dies at age 14. Cynthia Wesley dies at age 14. All under the collapse of brick, mortar, steel, and glass. More children and adults are injured. Families are torn apart.

Robert Chambliss, Bobby Cherry, and Thomas Blanton Jr. were convicted for the murders. Other suspects were never prosecuted. One of the town's White citizens, a young attorney at the time of the bombing, recalls how 122 sticks of dynamite were used in an attempt to destroy Black expression, resistance, and transformation:

> It was just an act of terrorism in my judgment, and those are the, in many ways, as we know today, the hardest ones to resolve and the cruelest, because they don't care who it is that gets killed, as long as there's some symbolism in what they're doing. (Lee & Pollard, 1997)

The bombing of Sixteenth Street Baptist Church adds to a sense of terror within the Black American psyche. Eight years prior to the Birmingham bombing, a jury acquitted two White men for the brutal murder of 14-year old Emmett Till. Till had been accused of whistling at a White woman. He was beaten, stabbed, and shot before his body was dumped into the Tallahatchie River. The White power structure—including the sheriff, coroner, and local media of Money, Mississippi—assisted in exonerating J. W. Milam and Roy Bryant from the murder of the Black child. Two years later, *Look Magazine* paid Milam and Bryant $4,000 for their confessions (Metress, 2002). Memories of Bull Connor, J. W. Milam, Roy Bryant, and others resurrect images of the "good ol' boy" networks that situate perpetrators as untouchable and in cahoots with a system of power. Representations of terror within critical memory infiltrate discourse of the present.

Four

VOICE

Speak to him? No one speaks to him. He does the speak-
ing—

—Ellison (1952, p. 142)

There was an energy bill on the floor of the Senate loaded
down with goodies, billions for the oil companies, and it
was sponsored by Bush and Cheney. You know who voted
for it? You might never know—that one.

—John McCain (2008,
quoted in www.washingtonwire.com)

Senate Majority Leader Harry Reid of Nevada encouraged
Mr. Obama to run early on, arguing that the country was
ready to embrace a Black presidential candidate, especial-
ly one such as Obama—"a light-skinned African American
with no Negro dialect, unless he wanted to have one."

—Heilemann and Halperin (2010, p. 37)

Thematic voice deals with verbal and written correctives, reconciliation, and challenges to oppressive power. Voice itself is a rhetorical construct consisting of words, language, oration, and narratives that develop and transform life. Essential qualities of voice include any given speech or text on matters of oppression. Voice is the articulation of a particular point of view. Voice imparts definitions of self. To speak is to establish voice. To have voice is to establish identity.

This chapter consists of three parts. Part I examines the process of speaking and naming Black identity into and out of existence. Part II focuses on a Black feminist approach to language and the rhetoric of affirmation relating to girlhood. Part III highlights the rhetoric of possibility in the Black voice.

PART I: NAMING OURSELVES

African American rhetorical traditions emphasize voice. For example, the power to name informs or omits voice. Throughout Ellison's (1952) text, Invisible Man goes without a name. Thus, the Black man is unnamed and unseen except through ascription by Whites. At one point, the Brotherhood assigns Invisible Man a name. Although the community organization claims to speak for society's dispossessed, it also replicates the dominant structure by ascribing identities to the poor. To accept the new identity requires Invisible Man to discard his original voice and replace it with a voice that more accurately reflects the organization's values. In return, Invisible Man is granted a weekly salary—a far cry from the poverty he has known. The transformation begins the moment Brother Jack hands him a slip of paper:

> That is your new name. Start thinking of yourself by that name from this moment. Get it down so that even if you are called in the middle of the night you will respond. . . . You are to respond to no other, understand? (Ellison, 1952, p. 235)

Invisible Man will do whatever is required to gain mobility. Within the Black experience, societal roles are resisted and created through naming. To accept a name is to accept an identity. Conversely, to be stripped of a name is to be stripped of identity.

In Richard Wright's (1945) case, the segregated train car is the setting for an early exploration of identity. As young Wright and his mother travel to Arkansas, their conversation reveals notions of identity based on naming. Thinking about his grandmother, Wright questions the ways in which names inform Black identity:

"What was Granny's name before she married Grandpa?"
"Bolden."
"Who gave her that name?"
"The White man who owned her."
"She was a slave?"
"Yes."
"And Bolden was the name of Granny's father?"
"Granny doesn't know who her father was."
"So they just gave her any name?"
"They gave her a name; that's all I know."
"Couldn't Granny find out who her father was?"
"For what, silly?"
"So she could know."
"Know for what?"
"Just to know."
"But for *what*?"
I could not say. I could not get anywhere.
"Mama, where did Father get his name?"
"From his father."
"And where did the father of my father get his name?"
"Like Granny got hers. From a White man."

(Wright, p. 1945, p. 57)

Wright's questions are not new. After emancipation, many ex-slaves took on the names of their former masters. Others "decided they 'had nuff o' old massa" (Bennett, 1968, p.181) and looked further for self-identification. Wright's questions concern the changing nature of identity. The prolific discussion suggests that language is interwoven with Black consciousness. Wright's father was given one name whereas his grandmother took on another. In his attempt to trace his past, Wright cannot get beyond the White man who named his family members. His is an intense search into the power of language. Within Western canons, rhetoric concerns the distribution of resources. Within African American rhetorical traditions, the power to name is equivalent to identity—one's most valuable resource.

Communicative acts work to express and transform Black consciousness. The search for identity begins with the question, "Who am I in relation to others?" Thus, it is not unusual that young Wright would attempt to answer the question in a single word. To name is to exercise power and create conditions for liberty.

Nommoic creativity is the idea that everything begins with the word. The word introduces new ideas and thoughts. It is fresh, innovative, and creative, and stretches for alternate meanings. Black communication is founded on the concept of nommo. It is the power to constitute and carry "being" into the internal, collective, and spiritual realms. Nommo came across the Atlantic Ocean with the first Africans. This concept continues to inform Black rhetoric, Black dialect, and Black culture. According to Alkebulan (2003), nommo is the power of language to arouse God. It comes from the deepest parts of human beingness in the form of breath and life, and is pregnant with human meaning. Nommo is not grounded in persuasion, but in giving and sharing lived experiences. These are the words that allow listeners to share in the moment. Birthed from African tradition, nommo is to express, resist, and transform life.

Wright's inquiry is revealing, but it is not new. The power to name and create has always been challenged throughout the Black American experience. Smitherman (2000) follows this history in *From Africa to African American*. In the 17th and 18th centuries, slave traders, owners, and overseers stripped Africans of their names for the purpose of recreating identity. The first step in creating slaves was to detach them physically and psychologically from their land, culture, and history. The word *slave* connotes the attempt to dehumanize the African. To control the mind is to control the action. In many ways removing one's name and assigning the label was the first step towards slavery.

Not all survivors succumbed to oppressive language as quickly. In resistance, the word *African* continued to be used by persons who desired to maintain their connection to the continent. These Africans understood the significance of self-identification and self-avowal through the use of their native languages. Next, the use of *colored* increased between the Revolutionary and Civil Wars. Although colored soldiers fought in both wars, they were not recognized as Americans. Throughout the South, colored signified a second-class citizenship. As the nation moved into the 20th century, W. E. B. Du Bois helped popularize the term *Negro* as a method of regaining a lost sense of identity and dignity.

Throughout the Civil Rights Movement and the Black Power Movement, *Black* was used to illustrate cultural and political change. Smitherman (2000) writes, "Black symbolized an ideological shift in the repudiation of Whiteness and the rejection of assimilation necessary to gain personal and political power" (p. 47). In the 1970s and 1980s, the popularity of *Afro American* and *African American* evoked an African past while laying claim to a rightful and deserving place in America. These names reveal a transformation in ideology. There has never been a time when all Black/African Americans accepted each transformation, but the terms serve as a rallying point for persons who share ancestral ties—just as the continent of Africa and its diverse culture symbolizes a common heritage for various groups.

Concomitantly, within classic narratives, *nigger* is an insulting reference largely meant to dehumanize people of African descent. Du Bois (as quoted in Asim, 2007) describes the strategy behind oppressive language:

> Personal disrespect and mockery, the ridicule and systemic humiliation, the distortion of fact and wanton license of fancy, the cynical ignoring of the better and the boisterous welcoming of the worse, the all-pervading desire to inculcate disdain for everything Black, from Toussaint to the devil. (p. 2)

Inherent to the n-word are centuries of terror, rape, and murder of countless human beings. The word reeks of hate. Ironically, at the dawn of the 21st century, the n-word began to take on precarious connotations reflecting myriad standpoints, locations, and experiences. Some Blacks (and Whites) even use the word to describe themselves. The results include public deliberations over language and its impact on self-image.

Ongoing debates mirror competing ideologies and diverse philosophies. When, in 2007, the NAACP held a symbolic funeral to officially bury the word, some argued that the move infringed upon rights to free speech. If critical language—like critical thought—contributes to freedom, they posited, we cannot afford to dismiss the valuable cultural significance apparent in the works of Toni Morrison, Maya Angelou, Richard Pryor, Dead Prez, and Nas—just to name a few.

Black Americans have always strived to resist and transform oppressive power. For example, Wright (1945) never bought into his demise: "My deepest instincts had always made me reject the place to which the White south had assigned me. It never occurred to me that I was in any way an inferior being" (p. 283). In the latter part of the 20th century, more than ever before, Blacks sought to transform the n-word and its many variations into a term of endearment. For example, hip-hop artists "A Tribe called Quest" illustrate this transformation process in their song "Sucka Nigga":

> See, nigga first was used back in the deep south
> Fallin out between the dome of the White man's mouth
> It means that we will never grow, you know the word dummy
> Other niggas in the community think it's crummy
> But I don't, neither does the youth cause we
> Embrace adversity it goes right with the race
> And being that we use it as a term of endearment
> Niggas start to bug to the dome is where the fear went
> Now the little shorties say it all of the time
> And a whole bunch of niggas throw the word in they rhyme
> Yo I start to flinch, as I try not to say it
> But my lips is like the oowop as I start to spray it . . .
>
> (Davis, Muhammad, Taylor, & Hubbard, 1993)

These lyrics exemplify the expression of a particular experience, the representation of social conditions, and the transformation of meaning. The M.C. resists oppression by claiming the n-word and throwing it back into the face of the oppressor. The word becomes a term of endearment in a community of Black communicators. Admittedly, the ethical struggles continue (i.e., the M.C. tries not to say the word, but does so anyway). The rhetorical acts of naming and renaming may appear extreme, but so too is the Black experience. The complexity of freedom is not to be taken lightly. The nature of self-consciousness is such that members of oppressed groups lay claim to pejorative terms.

The communication of identity begs the questions: How has voice mattered? How does language and naming matter? In 2008, the University of Central Florida's Institute for Diversity and Ethics in Sport reported that approximately 53% of all African American basketball players graduated from college; 37% of overall African American students graduated from college; and 53% of all African American students graduated from high school (America's Promise Alliance Report, 2008). Do these numbers suggest that language informs reality? Consider the ways in which Black identity is created and assigned by others. To what degree does self-image impact success or failure for Blacks in predominantly White societal structures?

PART II: A RHETORIC
OF AFFIRMATION

Part II continues the focus on voice by identifying rhetoric of affirmation in general, and aesthetics and ascension in Black girlhood specifically.

Voice is essential to integrate, organize, and maintain our home worlds. Voice includes the communicative acts through which knowledge about culture is passed. According to Dandy (1991), Black communication consists of style, speech acts, speech codes, moral teachings, rules, and behaviors—all of which construct meaning within the life of a community. Yet the shifting and changing nature of communication reflects the fact that reality is never the same for each member. This speaks to the ever-present rhetorical question, "Who am I in relation to those around me?"

The rhetorical voice serves to express and represent Black consciousness. For example, after recognizing the detrimental images associated with Black skin and hair, bell hooks reverses the polarity of mediated power for purposes of transforming Black girlhood. In hooks's (1999a) *Happy to be Nappy*, the author subverts racialized patriarchy by re-articulating race and gender. In the rich tradition of Black feminism, hooks draws from critical memories that "stay with me and appear and reappear in different shapes and forms in all my work" (hooks, 1996, p. xiv). Thus, *Happy to be Nappy* is a dedication to Black girlhood and a rhetoric of affirmation.

BLACK FEMINIST THOUGHT AND THE RHETORIC OF AFFIRMATION

> If you White you right
> If you Yellow you mellow
> If you Brown stick around
> If you Black, get back
> Way back!
>
> —Elaine Brown (1992)

Black feminist thought works to foreground ways in which race and gender matter in our daily lives. It resists White supremacist capitalist patriarchy and seeks economic, political, and ideological liberation for individuals and groups (hooks, 1999b). Here, I examine the popular images of skin tone, hair texture, and body type that contribute to ideological oppression for Black children, and call attention to hooks's (1999a) *Happy to be Nappy*—a children's book about aesthetic beauty and Black hair. Simultaneously this is a narrative about ascension and Black girlhood. As such I discuss Black feminist rhetoric's potential to reverse the polarity of mediated domination.

When Don Imus called members of the Rutgers University women's basketball team "nappy-headed hoes," he did so as one of the most recognizable voices on radio. Speaking to nearly 15 million listeners across 100 stations, Imus fueled popular perceptions of race and gender in the United States (Carter & Steinberg, 2007). In the aftermath, Imus tried to assuage the situation, arguing that Blacks make similar comments about themselves. Aside from his troubling misrepresentation of Black Americans, Imus failed to recognize the respect and trust necessary for in-group relationships. Consequently, some listeners interpret his words as a manifestation of, and contribution to, oppressive societal structures.

As a father, I am constantly reminded of the ways in which societal images attempt to constrict my children. These powerful words and images become more or less apparent depending on one's position in the social hierarchy. As was mentioned, I recall seeing this oppressive power when my daughter wished aloud to be White, because no one else in her kindergarten classroom had "Black hair or brown skin."

Children and adults alike are susceptible to subtle and detrimental representations of race (Hopson, 2009). The aforementioned conversation with my daughter took me back to a time when my son (at age five) made a similar comment—and beyond that to a critical memory of when I myself said the same thing to my father. If a picture is worth a thousand words, then scholars must scrutinize the incessant flow of racialized and gendered (mis)representations that permeate the globe.

For some Black/African American girls, identity construction can be a complex task (Boylorn, 2008; Spellers, 2002), particularly within a racialized society where children learn to associate Whiteness with value, and conversely devalue that which is not White (Bennett & Dickerson, 2001; hooks, 1996). Popular images of skin tone, hair texture, and body type have contributed to the oppression of Black girlhood (Christian, 1985; Cummings James, 2000; Hill Collins, 1990; hooks, 1996 & 1999b; Houston & Davis, 2002; James & Sharpley Whiting, 2000; Means Coleman, 2002). Within the United States, Black hair has a long history of being framed as inferior (Banks, 2000, Byrd & Tharps, 2001; Rooks, 2001; Spellers, 2002); and images of Whiteness are associated with beauty to the extent that Black girlhood is adversely affected (Christian, 1985).

Discussions concerning Black hair and childhood include the 1998 controversy surrounding a Brooklyn, N.Y. school teacher who read Carolivia Herron's (1997) *Nappy Hair* to a group of third-graders. After reading the book, the teacher, who is White, received numerous complaints from Black parents and community members. Much of the strife had to do with the book's title. Some argued that its references to nappy hair perpetuate a negative stereotype. However, an alternative view situates nappy hair as symbolic of the strength and fortitude of the Black experience.

In *Nappy Hair*, the protagonist is a little girl described as having the nappiest hair in the world. For some readers, the idea of nappy hair represents a derogatory stereotype of Black girlhood (Rooks, 2001). For others, nappy or kinky hair represents a distinguished Afrocentric past (Ebong, 2001). Explaining the significance of *Nappy Hair*, Herron calls the book a celebration of Black hair where nappy becomes a term of endearment and a form of resistance to the dominant culture.

In *Bone Black: Memories of Girlhood*, hooks (1996) recalls "good hair" as a popular expression among Black folk who value hair that is "straight, not kinky, and does not feel like balls of steel wool" (p. 91). Here, "good" equates to "White," and "kinky" equates to "bad" or "Black." Moreover, the author remembers Saturday evenings as a time of transformation, and a time when mothers pressed their daughters' hair with a hot comb. The conscious effort to straighten Black hair achieves two goals. The first goal is aesthetic beauty, hooks (1996) writes:

> Real good hair is straight hair, hair like White folk's hair. Yet no
> one says so. No one says your hair is so beautiful, so nice

because it is like White folk's hair. We pretend that the standards
we measure our beauty by are our own invention. (p. 91)

This quote suggests that pressing (straightening) Black hair is an effort
to meet standards for acceptance within White society. Conversely, as an
example of ascension, doing hair creates time for bonding. Getting one's
hair braided, plaited, or pressed is a time for girls and women to gath-
er together. "This is our ritual and our time. It is a time without men"
(hooks, 1996, p.92). Upon reaching adulthood hooks decides not to press
her hair and instead chooses to wear an afro. For hooks and others,
choosing to wear afros, naturals, and braids symbolizes noncompliance
with oppressive structures (Ebong, 2001) and communicates to the
dominant culture, "I don't go along with your philosophy, and I don't
care that you know" (Byrd & Tharp, 2001, p. 57).

Hair becomes intrinsically politicized for those who directly refute
White/European American standards of beauty that dominate popular
media. In *Hair Matters: Beauty, Power, and Black Women's
Consciousness*, Banks (2000) argues that, historically, nappy has been
considered a derogatory term used to minimize Black hair and Black
people. Likewise, Bennett and Dickerson (2001) discuss a social hierarchy within Black communities, created in part by polarized ideas about
light and dark skin, and good and bad hair.

Popular images impact Black girlhood to varying degrees. In the
essay "Wearing Your Race Wrong: Hair, Drama, and a Politics of
Representation for African American Women at Play on a Battlefield,"
Rooks (2001) remembers a middle school student whose peers and
teachers chastise her for not straightening her hair. Rooks attempts to
comfort the student, but offers the following perspective in hindsight:

I now wish I had merely told her that there have long been consequences within and outside of African American communities,
for wearing one's race wrong, and that hairstyles are often the
means others use to determine whether we are wearing a right,
or wrong, racial identity. (p. 280)

By focusing on controversies within academic, organizational, and societal structures, Rooks contributes to a collective effort to illustrate the
politicization of Black hair.

Elsewhere, in *Hair Story: Untangling the Roots of Black Hair in
America*, Byrd and Tharps (2001) argue that Black hair is a cultural
phenomenon: "The story of Black hair begins where everything begins,
in Africa" (p. 2). The authors assert that frizzy, curly, kinky, and nappy
hair is the natural response to the unique African climate and culture.
Beyond protection from the sun's rays, Black hair is the act of expres-

sion. In ancient African civilizations—age, identity, wealth, and rank could be identified by hairstyle. Furthermore, groups inhabiting specific geographic regions could be identified by hair. Within the African tradition, hair is a highly rhetorical act.

Children's books which foreground the historical significance of braids and cornrows (Yarbrough, 1979), locks (DeVeaux, 1987), and nappy hair (Herron 1997; hooks, 1999a) may contribute to knowledge and self-worth in Black girls. Indeed, perceptions of self must be measured in relation to the distinct experience of girlhood; hooks (1996) writes:

> An outspoken girl might still feel that she is worthless because her skin was not light enough or her hair the right texture. These are the variables that White researchers may not consider when they measure the self-esteem of Black females with a yardstick that was designed based on values emerging from the White experience. . . . To understand the complexity of Black girlhood we need more work that documents that reality in all its variations and diversity. (xiii)

Black girls continue to face potential domination in social hierarchies based largely on race, gender, and age. As a result, scholars write to express, resist, and transform that reality. The following paragraphs explore Black feminist thought in hooks's (1999a) story of Black hair and girlhood.

BLACK FEMINIST THOUGHT IN *HAPPY TO BE NAPPY*

Black feminist thought can be traced through the words of women enslaved in the South and their contemporaries in the North (Houston & Davis, 2002). This was an active response to an early feminist agenda that largely negated the impact of race and class. As such, Black feminist scholarship continues to focus on the lived experiences of Black women (Abel, Christian, & Moglen, 1997; Allen, 1996; Hill Collins, 1990), and prioritize these unique perspectives for theoretical and practical purposes.

Black feminist thinking emphasizes the importance of multiple truths and seeks to identify and communicate a liberation movement more representative of women of color. It is both a method and means to demystify oppressive structures (Hill Collins, 1990). Here, scholars write with overlapping purposes (1) to order their own thoughts and experiences; (2) to make connections with other Black women and the larger society; and (3) to use energy to transform the world (Christian, 1985).

The Black experience includes various ideas about how to address ideological oppression, including narratives that encourage self-esteem in young readers. Skin tone and hair texture have long held a distinct social meaning for Black Americans (Banks, 2000). Skin tone and hair texture were used as social markers throughout slavery and beyond. Consequently, physical features associated with Whiteness were characterized as valuable, whereas features associated with Blackness were characterized largely as picayune (Banks, 2000). In *Happy to be Nappy,* hooks (1999a) embraces the concept of nappy. Recognizing the oppressive binary of Black/White, bad/good, ugly/pretty, inferior/superior, and sad/happy, hooks transforms nappy, and in the process transforms notions of Black girlhood.

The simple yet strategic title frames Black hair as a happy thing, in opposition to the less flattering image of Blackness found within the aforementioned quote by Elaine Brown. From cover to cover, hooks's (1999a) narrative repeatedly associates nappy hair with beauty, in the same way that popular media has long associated straight, blonde hair with happiness and beauty. *Happy to be Nappy* is a story about hair, but a Black feminist critique reveals much more that that.

BLACK HAIR AS AESTHETIC

> Girlpie hair smells clean and sweet
> Is soft like cotton
> Flowery petal billowy soft
> Full of frizz and fuzz
>
> —hooks (1999a, pp. 1– 4)

Although popular stereotypes portray Black hair as wrong or bad, hooks constructs Black hair as a source of pride. Her story moves rhythmically like a song or poem that conjures visual, olfactory, and tactile imagery of Black hair as something to be admired. The first verse reads, "Girlpie hair smells clean and sweet" (p. 1), while an illustration of a pretty brown face smiles pleasantly. Assorted colors decorate the ends of her braided hair. Could this be the face of Girlpie? Does the face represent Black girlhood? Perhaps both are true.

> A halo~a crown~
> A covering for heads that are round
> It can be smooth or patted down

> Pulled tight, cut close
> Or just let go
> So wind can carry it all over the place
> Hair to comb, Hair to brush
> To twist and plait or just lie flat
>
> —hooks (1999a, pp. 5–12)

Girlpie's emergence contradicts a history of linguistic erasure. Raschka's colorful illustration brings each verse to life. The first half of the narrative frames Black girlhood as aesthetically appealing. Within these pages, hooks speaks of Black hair as clean, sweet, and soft to the touch, especially when worn "smooth or patted" (p. 7), "tight and close" (p. 8), "plaited" (p.12), and "locked, twisted, and curled" (p. 28). In the process Black girlhood is versatile and creative. It is smiling, laughing, doting, proud, alive, and happy. Various shades of brown represent varying strands of Black feminist thought. Throughout *Happy to Nappy*, Black girlhood is beautifully and collectively human.

Next, Black hair is associated with the possibility for ascension. This possibility goes back to Africa where hair signified age, occupation, clan, and status (Banks, 2000). Herron (1997) describes nappy hair as "an act of God that came through Africa" (p. 12). Black hair is spiritual, beautiful, and purposeful. When hooks (1999a) covers Black hair with a halo, young readers learn that Black girlhood is good, angelic, and divine. Black hair is a crown that symbolizes a royal African history, just as it is a natural cover and protection for precious heads.

> Hair for hands to touch and play!
> Hair to take the gloom away
> Sitting still for hands to brush or braid
> And make the days start hopefully
> All kinks gone! All heads of joy!
> These short tight naps
> Or plaited strands all
> Let girls go running free
> Happy to be nappy!
> Happy with hair all short and strong
> Happy with locks that twist and curl
> Just all girl happy!
> Happy to be nappy hair!
>
> —hooks (1999a, pp. 13–30)

When hooks writes "hair to comb, hair to brush" (p. 11), "hair for hands to touch and play" (pp. 13 & 14), and "sitting still for hands to brush or

braid" (p. 17), the author is referring to a special time of bonding, transformation, and beautification. The notion of spending time is further
supported by an image of a mother standing and smiling while brushing
her daughter's hair. This represents the bond between mother and
daughter. While mother tends to daughter's hair, stories are shared, cultures are formed, and generations interact with one another. At some
point in their lives the daughter will tend to her mother's hair. Als (2001)
describes this generational interaction as an emotional and intellectual
exchange among women. Additionally, in *Bone Black*, hooks (1996)
referred to the ritual in this way:

> We are comforted by the parting hands that comb and braid,
> comforted by the intimacy and bliss. There is a deeper intimacy
> in the kitchen on Saturday, when hair is pressed, when fish is
> fried, when sodas are passed around, when soul music drifts
> over the talk. We are women together. (p. 92)

The qualities of Black hair are many. Recalling the special time, hooks
frames Black girlhood as having its own beautiful culture and traditions.
Black hair is angelic, proud, and enjoyable to touch, brush, and braid.
Each verse supplies the reader with tools for constructing self-esteem
and self-worth.

BLACK HAIR AS ASCENSION

Beyond aesthetics, hooks (1999a) emphasizes the intrinsic qualities of
Black hair. A sense of community is established around girlhood
through illustrations of girls playing and laughing together. Images of
Black women interacting with Black girls establish the significance of
intergenerational relationships. These relationships are essential to
girlhood if one is to know how to react in any circumstance (Cooper,
1994).

The images in *Happy to be Nappy* transcend physical and mental
boundaries. One illustration features Girlpie leaning into the blowing
wind. As she resists the force of the wind, Black girlhood is encouraged
to "just let go so wind can carry it all over the place" (p. 9). The act of
letting go is symbolic of freeing herself from the hegemonic forces that
seek to restrict Black girlhood.

To be clear, this subtle message does not imply giving in, but resists
being defined by the struggle. Hence, the battle does not belong to
Girlpie. She is free to take her energy elsewhere, to use it in a different
manner. The words of freedom declare: "let girls go running free" (p.
24). Five girls play together, all different shades of brown, wearing

locks, braids, twists, and plaits. Emancipation is signified by a collage of colorful shapes and figures which together rise above oppression. There is strength in collectivity, strength in Black hair, and strength in Black girlhood.

Happy to be Nappy works to transcend racism, sexism, and ageism. The narrative opposes negative stereotypes. Instead, these words are positive: "hair to take the gloom away" (p.16), "to make the day start hopefully" (p. 18); to adorn "heads of joy" (p. 20), and "just all girl happy" (p. 29). By constructing Black hair as hopeful, joyful, and happy, hooks nurtures the self-esteem of those who, historically and socially, have been positioned as the *other* and pushed to the outer margins of society.

When my daughter became concerned about being the only Black girl in her classroom, she asked the questions that I believe are relevant to all marginalized individuals and groups. A conscious connection to the world enables one to participate more fully in the creation of that world. Black feminist thought illuminates the restrictions that discourage and impede societal participation. Surely the United States continues to be a racialized and gendered society to the extent that children are taught that skin tone, hair texture, body type, and overall physical appearance are associated with human value. Understanding that Whiteness has been associated with beauty, pride, worth, and freedom, hooks (1999a) works to express, resist, and transform the narrative of Black girlhood.

Regarding the limitations here, I recognize that girlhood cannot be explicated fully in one discussion about hair. Nor can economic, political, and ideological inequities be remedied with a children's book. I do not assume that understanding any lived experience is such a simple process. However, I think it is important to extend the discussion beyond the characters and comments espoused in popular media. We must move from sensitivity to accountability. Don Imus's flippant remarks were pointless. But the shock jock informs almost 15 million listeners daily, reportedly commands nearly 10 million dollars in annual salary, and returned to radio after 8 months of suspension (Carter & Steinberg, 2007)—all of which suggest a method to the madness.

Part II delineated some of the sociohistorical forces that impact Black girlhood and revealed rhetorical strategies that challenge racialized patriarchy. By emphasizing the intrinsic beauty of Black hair, hooks's narrative promotes the primary themes of aesthetics and ascension. In writing this particular children's story, hooks contributes to the pride and self-worth of readers. Throughout the narrative, Black hair and Black girlhood are expressed and transformed in ways understandable to children and adults.

Stories enlarge the possibilities for voice, particularly among non-dominant group members historically alienated from dominant society.

Voice is synonymous with emancipation. Narratives work to address, confront, deconstruct, and interrogate a dominant language system that has denied difference and muted diverse voices. Black communicators share epistemic struggles. Individuals use voice to make sense of their lives. Within hooks's (1999a) book, the Black voice resists stereotypical messages and transforms oppression into aesthetics and ascension. In this way, hooks relies on the rhetoric of affirmation.

Our interactions help to establish a meaningful life world and give order to the human experience. Individual interpretations of the human experience contribute to a diverse society in general and a deeper understanding within the communication discipline in particular. In this capacity, theorizing through story telling extends understanding about communication, culture, and societal structures.

The Black experience happens through myriad times and tongues. Because these stories are produced in the midst of domination, narratives concerning the Black experience gain significance when considering the risks and sacrifices made by rhetors. Recall the times when reading and writing could result in serious injury or worse, and the extent to which literacy contributes to voice becomes clearer. It is for this reason that Black communication includes a rhetoric of possibility.

PART III: VOICE AND A RHETORIC
OF POSSIBILITY

> I stood up, trying to realize what reality lay behind the meaning of words. . . . Yes, this man was fighting, fighting with words. He was using words as a weapon, using them as one would use a club. Could words be weapons? Well, yes, here they were. Then, maybe, perhaps, I could use them as a weapon?
>
> —Wright (1945, p. 272)

In Part III, I examine voice that occurs through literacy, language, and protest. Undoubtedly, hooks, Wright, and Ellison use functional art to express, resist, and transform inequalities of 20th century America. This practice continues today. Within African-centered philosophy, it is known as the rhetoric of possibility.

Wright (1945) remembers when Blacks were prohibited from reading and writing. The communicator recalls when laws against literacy served to squelch Black voice. Slave owners believed that illiterate slaves developed fewer ideas about freedom. Parker Pool, an ex-slave, remembers, "No, sirree, dey wouldn't let us have no books. Dey would not let none o' de chilluns tell us anything about a book" (Howell, 2004b,

p. 57). At the dawn of the 20th century, literacy came with a great risk. The tensions would remain embedded in the Black American psyche for decades to come.

As Wright develops an interest in reading, he hides his books from his White co-workers. Hiding his books is part of a larger strategy to manage visibility and avoid retaliation. Wright knows that reading while Black is cause for terror. Nonetheless, a White co-worker loans him a library card. This is dangerous because Blacks are expected to feign ignorance for their own well-being. Wright notes a time when Black communicators avoid controversial topics such as the 13th, 14th, and 15th amendments, communism, socialism, and any manly self-assertion on the part of the Negro. One's safety depends on how well he can conceal his feelings. He will continue the practice of hiding his books, and his voice, well into adulthood.

Within early stages of his awakening, Wright is faced with a bevy of moods and ideas. He develops a growing distance from Negro life as he has known it. He is taken by the revelation that words contain the power of ascension. This newfound consciousness prompts Wright to develop his own voice. Though ridden with tension and anxiety, he will use reading and writing to better understand his condition. Wright sets his sights on a new life in the North.

Elsewhere, Invisible Man has his own revelation concerning the rhetoric of possibility. While in Harlem, NY, he sees a poor family being evicted from their home. When the elderly woman is refused permission to say a final prayer, the crowd becomes irate. Someone yells, "They're against us!" Another person yells, "Take your hands off that woman!" Still, another resists, "Think you can come up here and hit one of our women, you a fool!" At this point Invisible Man uses what he calls the "magic in spoken words" to speak out against the injustice:

> They don't want the world, but only Jesus. They only want Jesus, just fifteen minutes of Jesus on the rug-bare floor. . . . How about it Mr. Law? Do we get our fifteen minutes worth of Jesus? You got the world, can we have our Jesus? (Ellison, 1952, p. 211)

Invisible Man's words contribute to a protest universe where common experiences, truths, and understanding unite the audience. The formation of unity is the result of a mutual cause and based in the realm of possibility. Possibility is required to transform inequitable social conditions. Acting against societal conditions requires the Black communicator to use prevailing behaviors and hearerships to call on the people (Asante, 1998). Here, inspirational words include "Jesus" and "law." The common experience is oppression. Each communicator knows these elements in her or his own way. The bond is strengthened with every word spoken.

Moreover, the Black communicator relies on irony. There is a degree of cynicism in calling the evictors "Mr. Law." Law should imply righteousness or good, but Invisible Man constructs the eviction process as bad. Here, law represents an unfair system. The eviction is symbolic of dominant structures where the dispossessed and disenfranchised are kicked out and forgotten. Invisible Man drives the point home: "Just look at their possessions in the snow. How old are you, sir? Did you hear him? He's eighty-seven. Eighty-seven and look at all he's accumulated in eighty-seven years" (p. 210). Irony is made clear. Their anger intensifies. "Strewn in the snow like chicken guts, and we're a law-abiding, slow-to-anger bunch of folks turning the cheek every day in the week." With every word, Invisible Man transforms law into lawlessness. Eventually, in a last act of resistance, he convinces the onlookers to put the elderly couple's belongings back into the home.

One can imagine Invisible Man's sermonic protests. He draws from a spiritual voice that has united African descendants for centuries, "'We're dispossessed,' I sang at the top of my voice." The idea of a new beginning creates possibility among the people. The audience trusts a speaker in tune with God. In righting the wrongs of the dominant system, the Black communicator represents a righteous force. Invisible Man's speech flows from the heart. Tone and pronunciation work together to maintain a liberating effect of oneness. The spoken word invites the audience to join in. Voices in the crowd cry out in response: "Hell no, he ain't lying." "Naw, suh!"

Words and actions create balance in life's rhythm. Good bequeaths good. Oppositional forces are addressed by any means necessary. The protest speaker calls forth and inspires memories of a historical and spiritual journey. The words touch, activate, and resonate with the audience. By defining oppression and presenting liberation the Black communicator produces a rhetoric of possibility.

SUMMARY

This chapter explored Black voice. Voice for marginalized individuals and groups reveals how power is enacted discursively. The act of naming, for example, may inform identity. To remove or replace a name is to alter identity. This history goes back to American slavery, but critical memory bears witness today. For example, recall the 2008 presidential debate when Sen. John McCain referred to Sen. Barack Obama as "that one." Consider the following discussion questions: Was McCain's comment an intercultural/interracial issue? What does "that one" mean in terms of cultural and/or racial competence? Moreover, recall the words of Sen. Reid as quoted in the beginning of this chapter, did the prediction that "America was ready for a Black president with light skin and no Negro dialect"—speak truth to power? Did dialect work to the advantage of either candidate?

Black feminist thought examines the ever increasing dynamics of race, gender, class, and age. In this chapter, the rhetoric of affirmation informs aesthetics and ascension in Black girlhood. The rhetoric of possibility includes literacy, language, and protest within intercultural contexts. Voice is an overarching theme in Black communication. To diminish or deny voice is to negate the experience. Silence contributes to the linguistic erasure of nondominant groups. Silence represents someone or something missing. Silence reinforces the dominant ideology. With voice we disrupt silence.

Five

SPACE

A variety of communities are now beginning to interrogate the sources, discursive spaces, and material realities that influence all of our perceptions concerning social relationships.

—Hasian and Nakayama (1998)

With ever watching eyes and bearing scars, visible and invisible, I headed North, full of a hazy notion that life could be lived with dignity.

—Wright (1945)

I have suggested that critical memory within classic texts allows the reader to vicariously experience the world from a unique vantage-point. Wright, hooks, Ellison and others have spoken with great clarity to issues surrounding intercultural and interracial communication. In this chapter, I apply their ideas to my own academic experiences. The chapter consists of two parts. In Part I, I conceptualize rhetorical space. In Part II, I examine my own Black communicative experience within Whitespace.

PART I: SPACE AND THE COLOR-LINE

The iterativity of space illuminates the ways in which context, situation, and environment can empower or disempower communicators. Positioning Black communication as intercultural communication requires examination of historic space because the (in)ability to control the environment has always held great significance for individuals and groups. Physical and psychological space exists all around us. I consider the African Diaspora as a process of transporting slaves from one space to another. Colonization is the occupation of space. Also, think about restricted movement resulting from Jim Crow laws. One cannot overlook the manipulation of space via sit-ins and marches of the Civil Rights Movement. We might debate whether the psychic space of possibility increased when an African American man assumed the highest office in the land, or when a Hispanic woman ascended to the highest court in the land.

Societies are the result of space classifications. Constant and politically charged deliberations have resulted in space investigations, land development, and land preservation. Cities, countries, and continents are divided into territorial spaces, and human beings are often identified by the spaces we inhabit. Space is associated with freedom and liberty. Conversely, denied freedoms reflect denied access to space. Exploring space as a sociohistoric phenomenon requires that we explore the intercultural and interracial spaces of yesterday.

During the Civil War, the Mason-Dixon Line was seen as a distinguishing marker between slave states and free states. Black life hinged on this color-line. The American South maintained slavery longer than the American North so the color-line represented the difference between slavery and freedom. Many Blacks risked life and limb to make it North. To uphold slavery, Southern states restricted the physical movement of Blacks. For example, Blacks had to possess freedom papers that served as evidence that freedom had been purchased. In other cases, Black slaves could travel only with written permission from slave owners. Mobility came by way of a written pass listing ownership and the name, date, and destination for the slave who otherwise risked being punished or kidnapped by patrollers who turned runaway slaves into financial gain.

In *I was a Slave* (Howell, 2004b), Daniel William Lucas remembers the time when Black slaves fled the South in search of freedom. In the face of great danger several Blacks escaped while others did not. At the dawn of the Civil War, runaways increased as Blacks attempted to join the Union Army. A former slave recalls the hefty price for crossing the color-line:

> Maybe some of them would make for the North. They was the lucky ones 'cause lots of times they was caught. When the patrollers get 'em caught, they was due for a heavy licking [whipping] that would last for a long time. The slaves didn't know how to travel. The way would be marked when they'd start North, but somehow they'd get lost cause they didn't know one direction from another. They was so scairt. Just like yesterday, I remember. (Howell, 2004b, p. 48)

Space has long been used to control Black bodies. As noted, Blacks often risked everything to escape the Southern plantation. In the absence of formal directions, some relied on the North Star.

Elsewhere, Solomon Northup (1968), an ex-slave, describes a slave owner who reads Bible passages aloud in order to construct the peculiar institution of slavery as natural and ordained. Northup observes how slave owners use the Holy Bible to justify human bondage. Deceptive interpretations of Bible passages became a way to create obedience and passivity in Blacks, urging them to wait on a better world and a better place which would come by way of heaven. The message forbade Blacks from resistance and demonstrated the subtle power of re-articulating space on the plantation.

The plantation itself served to situate slaves physically and psychologically in hierarchical order. Blacks working within the slave-owner's home were known as house slaves and seen as obtaining a quality of life higher than Blacks who lived and worked in the fields—field slaves. Living and working closer to the slave owner's house meant access to better food, clothing, and information. Life as a slave also differed depending on one's skin tone. A common belief is that field slaves were often darker skinned, whereas house slaves had lighter complexions as the result of miscegenation initiated by slave owners.

Life on the plantation was better for those closest to Whiteness. Kate Curry, a former slave, reports "Massa had his own house servants . . . like de coachman, de stable boy, and de body servant for himself" (Howell, 2004a, p. 20). Thomas Campbell remembers, "Marse James was a great lawyer in dis day. I was his houseboy and office boy. When I get older, I take on, besides blackin' of his boots and shoes and sweepin' de office, de position of carriage driver and sweepin' out de church" (p. 24). Additionally, Ben Chambers articulates privilege associated with Whiteness, "I drive de kerrige to carry de White folks to chu'ch on Sunday. . . . Dat was one of de bestes' tasks on de plantation and some of dem other niggers was sorter jealous of me" (p. 23).

On the other hand, ex-field slaves describe a different life. Jane Anne Privette Upperman reveals past hardships, "Mother said she worked in de fiel's from sun to sun" (p. 16). Henrietta McCullers remembers, "I plowed an' dug ditches an' cleaned new groun'." And Thomas Johns recalls the interlocking consequences of space and race, "My father was very Black. He was about six feet, two inches, and one of de strongest, hardest wukin' men I ever see. . . . It look like dey could jus' chop cotton all day widout stoppin" (p. 15). The rhetorical construction of space during slavery would influence Black-White communication for generations to come.

After emancipation, freedom was closely associated with land. In the 1870s, Paps Singleton urged Black Southerners to migrate to Kansas for economic independence and autonomy (Entz, 2003). During the 1920s, Marcus Garvey called for a Back-to-Africa movement, believing that Blacks could never gain independence without first owning land. In the 1960s, Elijah Muhammad demanded land as reparations for slavery. Throughout U.S. history, physical and theoretical space has held a special significance for Black Americans.

Arguably, plantation-like structures are reflected in today's societal formations. White skin, speech codes, and identity are still viewed as more valuable than non-White identifiers. Communities, neighborhoods, and areas associated with Whiteness often hold higher property values and presumed qualities of life (Delgado & Stefancic, 2001). Conversely, neighborhoods, communities, cities, and countries associated with anything other than Whiteness are viewed as less valuable. Critical memory is concerned with the ways in which organizational, institutional, and societal contexts inform intercultural interactions.

STRATEGIZING SPACE

Oppressive space contributes to feelings of helplessness and deficiency for Black communicators. Space is racialized to the extent that it impacts one's productivity. For example, when working around Southern Whites, Wright (1945) is incessantly preoccupied with curbing impulses, speech, movements, and manners of expression that cross the color-line. His strategy is to become less Black. As his anxieties increase, Wright finds himself concentrating excessively on menial tasks. He is unable to operate comfortably and confidently in the workplace. The Black communicator recognizes that his success is incumbent upon his image. The result is a fluctuating inability to adapt.

When Wright (1945) decides to leave the South, he devises a strategy to meet opposition from dominant group members. First, Wright gives just 2 days' notice in hopes of minimizing confrontation. Next,

Wright poses as an "innocent boy" (p. 278) who is leaving for Chicago only because he needs to accompany his paralyzed mother. Racialized space constricts his every word. The boss is like an overseer who can unravel Wright's plans at any given moment. Thus, Wright keeps a "neutral tone" (p. 279) and attempts to create "the impression that I was not asserting my will" (p. 278). Any show of strength or self-pride could interfere with Wright's plan to escape with his facilities in tact.

Getting beyond the boss is one step toward freedom, but Wright must also explain himself repeatedly to co-workers who resent his leaving. As the word spreads, Wright is approached over and over again. His co-workers begin to interrogate him:

> "How're you going to act up there?"
> "Just like I act down here, sir."
> "Would you speak to a White girl up there?"
> "Oh, no, sir, I'll act there just like I act here."
> "Aw, no, you won't. You'll change. Niggers change when they go North."
> I wanted to tell him that I was going North precisely to change, but I did not. "I'll be the same," I said, trying to indicate that I had no imagination whatsoever. As I talked I felt that I was acting out a dream. I did not want to lie, yet I had to lie to conceal what I felt. A White censor was standing over me and, like dreams forming a curtain for the safety of sleep, so did my lies form a screen of safety for my living moments. (Wright, 1945, p. 280)

Here, the Black communicator balances the tensions and strategies of racialized space. His strategy is to respond in bits and pieces. He will share the least amount of personal information. There is no denying the pressure. The Black communicator's escape hinges on his strategy.

Elsewhere, Invisible Man distinguishes between spaces of oppression. For example, he describes the freedom of eating yams on the streets of Harlem. Back in the South, he would have been hesitant to eat yams for fear of negative stereotypes of country Negroes. In the North, he does not worry as much about the stereotype. Biting into the yam, Invisible Man is overcome by an intense feeling of freedom:

> If only someone who had known me at school or at home would come along and see me now. How shocked they'd be! I'd push them into a side street and smear their faces with the peel. What a group of people we were, I thought. Why you could cause us the greatest humiliation simply by confronting us with something we liked. (Ellison, 1952, p. 200)

During the great migration, Blacks took with them food, music, and religion that would influence the Northern states for generations to come. However, as Invisible Man suggests, these Southern influences often came with a lot of baggage.

The Black communicator works to avoid stereotypes. In the North, he claims good old fashioned yam eating as a birthright. It is a dialectal tension associated with racialized space. Invisible Man remembers how prestigious Blacks like Dr. Bledsoe, the schoolmaster, denied their down-home ways in the presence of Whites. This kind of strategic dissociating is meant to separate the Black communicator from negative and demeaning stereotypes. Invisible Man imagines the pleasure of exposing Dr. Bledsoe and other Blacks who discriminate against their Southern ways: "Bledsoe, you're a shameless chitterling eater! I accuse you of relishing hog bowels! Ha! And not only do you eat them, you sneak and eat them in private!"

The Black communicator will search for a safer environment. Wright goes to Chicago. Invisible Man goes to Harlem. The turn of the 20th century found many Black Americans migrating North in pursuit of industry jobs and civil freedoms not found in the South. Many people were attracted to cities like Chicago and New York because of their growing Black populations. The North symbolized greater opportunity and fewer incidents of hostility and degradation. Although racism was not uncommon in the North, Blacks increasingly relocated at the advice of family members and friends. With the advent of White flight, Harlem witnessed an increased Black population making it the Negro capital of the world (Hine, Hine, & Harrold, 2003). This transformation ignited a time and space known as the Harlem Renaissance.

> Oh, to be in Harlem again after two years away.
> The deep-dyed color, the thickness,
> The closeness of it.
> The noise of Harlem, the sugared laughter.
> The honey-talk on its streets.
> And all night long, ragtime and blues
> playing somewhere . . . singing somewhere,
> dancing somewhere!
>
> —McKay (1928/2003)

Claude McKay's (1928/2003) *Home to Harlem* demonstrates how space served to empower Blacks in the early 20th century. Consequently, the struggle for civil rights remains an undeniable struggle for space. Part II extends previous discussions by placing space within the context of my own intercultural experiences.

PART II: INTERPRETING EXPERIENCES
AND MOVING TOWARD ETHNORELATIVISM

This moment—the one you are experiencing right now—is the culmination of all the moments you've experienced in the past. This moment is as it is because the entire universe is as it is.

—Chopra (1994, p. 57)

21ST CENTURY REMEMBRANCES OF SPACE

A student invaded my space today. Actually he invaded my space last week, but I gave him the benefit of the doubt then. Today he invaded my space again when he very well could have played it cool. After receiving yet another chance, he chose to insult me as I passed out the assignments, *"What's up bro!"*

For all intensive purposes, that student imposed upon my personal and professional space, which quickly led to a struggle for power. He had threatened the respect I worked so hard to gain in that classroom. At first I questioned whether I had been too friendly. But at that point there was nothing to be gained from second-guessing. I knew something had to be done. I would not continue in that direction. I had to regain my space. I quickly responded by telling that student—in so many words— to cease with the disrespect, loud enough for others to hear. There could be no mistake. I refuse to give up my space of respect, as an instructor and as a human being.

—Hopson (2007)

I was a teaching assistant at the time of this incident. During my time with this particular class, I took an interest in its rhetorical constructions. I paid close attention to how students organized themselves, including where people sat, who spoke to whom, and the manner in which daily practices were carried out. In addition, I became curious about the ways in which my race and gender seemed to influence (or not) this class of predominantly White students. I wondered whether some comments and actions resulted from their perceptions of me as a Black man, and I contemplated whether I made more of these issues than necessary. Consequently, I began to interrogate some of the ways that I (sub)consciously adjusted my body to that environment. I realize that in the classroom, and in a largely racialized U.S. society, I often feel locked into the Black body.

Later, I shared the experience with my colleague Jennifer who suggested that regaining symbolic space is especially strategic for women as well. After engaging in her own power struggles, Jennifer found it challenging to return to a space of comfort. She explained how some women within the academy become regulated to oppressive spaces. For example, sometimes after voicing her opinions in classrooms and faculty meetings, she felt stereotyped as "the bitch." After our conversation I thought about other times when I felt stereotyped and regulated within academia. I considered ways in which oppressive space reveals and conceals privilege; and encourages and discourages, enables and constrains, and empowers and disempowers group members on various levels. I concluded that it would be helpful and perhaps therapeutic to extend ideas concerning the dynamics of racialized bodies and space.

I see power as an enabling force or a web of relations that occurs with the occupation of space. Racialized space is where bodies infected by racist ideologies engage in power relationships which contribute to a larger whole. Consequently, a critique of racialized space must speak to geographical and theoretical formations of power within intercultural interactions, particularly in instances where Black communicators function in predominantly White settings. Black communicators juggle tensions and strategies within organizational, institutional, and societal structures. Critical memory illustrates how power enables and constrains individuals in communication situations. Our societal locations influence our interactions, making the space of communication a dynamic phenomenon. My teaching experience includes ongoing power negotiations. I recognize that a hierarchy exists wherein dominant group members occupy positions of societal power. These dominant practices sometimes impede upon nondominant members who are then forced into marginality.

The communication strategies I employed in the aforementioned classroom situation include confronting, educating others, and communicating self. I found that instructors occupy dominant and nondominant positions simultaneously. As an instructor, I maintain power. However, as a Black man at a predominantly White university, my role is sometimes challenged and compromised by students and faculty. Power is linked to the occupation of societal space, and prompts questions concerning the way in which cultural members represent and are represented by the spaces we inhabit.

Growing up, my peers and I believed that moving within 3 inches of one's face was a severe infringement upon personal space. During times of conflict, the invasion of personal space was taken as a sign of disrespect. Later, when I began working as staff person in an inner-city high school, I noticed a teacher who repeatedly broke the rule. The teacher had good intentions but lacked cultural knowledge concerning personal space. Clearly, the largely Black student population disapproved of the White teacher's oversight. Among the discontented group of students was Floyd Mayweather Jr.—who later became a 1996 Olympic medal winner and world boxing champion. With hopes of diffusing tension, I quickly brought the matter to the teacher's attention. Needless to say he agreed that our discussion held great pragmatic value.

Returning to my experience in the college classroom, the rhetorical construction of space takes on a new significance. When the student crossed my boundary of respect, I felt the need to reinforce my position. I confronted him. The act was both natural and informed. Confronting is a necessary and sometimes aggressive technique (Orbe, 1998). In my case, I addressed the student in front of his peers to make the point that I am not willing to be disrespected in that way. Of course, tensions could have escalated had the student felt the need to save face. But it was worth the risk at that time. After class I spoke with the student again and reminded him about the importance of respect. We parted ways with a general understanding. This was my attempt to educate him, whereby co-cultural group members accept the role of teacher to enlighten dominant group members on cultural norms and values.

Foucault (1980) said that power moves between the self and others. I have found this to be true. Space, for me, is created through communication and manipulated to establish positions of power within the classroom and larger society. After my classroom experience, I wondered if my students questioned the motives of their Black teacher. I also pondered whether students second-guess themselves with historical and cultural dialogues. Rather, do students see communication as a struggle for power? According to some colleagues, I am not alone in these questions. Strategizing space can be a time consuming practice for those of us who know racism or sexism too well.

To question the impact of space is to rediscover intercultural communication. Space—like race and gender—is created and maintained by dominant societal structures. I am in interested in how rhetorical bodies occupy and simultaneously create space. Corporeality itself is a site of knowledge and power (McKerrow, 1998), which is why it is fair to say that intercultural communication informs, and is informed by, space.

RACE, PRIVILEGE, AND WHITESPACE

In previous chapters we examined the space of privilege. For McIntosh (1988), White privilege is an invisible knapsack of unearned assets. She suggests that eliminating privilege requires a conscious move towards reflection and accountability. Another sample of McIntosh's (1988) list encourages learners to reflect on our respective experiences:

- I can go shopping alone most of the time, pretty well assured that I will not be followed or harassed.
- I can turn on the television or open to the front page of the paper and see people of my race widely represented.
- I can swear, or dress in second-hand clothes, or not answer letters, without having people attribute these choices to the bad morals, the poverty, or the illiteracy of my race.
- If a traffic cop pulls me over or if the IRS audits my tax return, I can be sure I haven't been singled out because of my race.
- I can go home from most meetings of organizations I belong to feeling somewhat tied in, rather than isolated, out-of-place, out-numbered, unheard, held at a distance, or feared.
- I can take a job with an affirmative action employer without having coworkers on the job suspect that I got it because of my race. (p. 2)

These examples illustrate the distance and disparity between privilege and denied-privilege. Spaces of privilege consist of micro and macro-practices that reinforce the status quo and work against nondominant groups. White privilege exemplifies a theoretical space of entitlement, freedom, and self-esteem. Conversely, non-Whites who enter this space may experience fear, self-doubt and anxiety. The subtle and dehumanizing dimension of space may surpass any overt acts of oppression.

I argue that Whitespace is the product of privilege and racialized space. In doing so, I draw from Moon's (1999) essay, "White enculturation and bourgeois ideology," which calls for thick descriptions of the diverse ways in which Whiteness works as a system of domination. Moon asserts that social constructions of Whiteness include linguistic shifts into a kind of "White code" that renders the status quo as natural and removes Whites from any evidence of complicity.

Moon (1999) also calls attention to coded speech which she calls "Whitespeak," where what is not said is more revealing than what is said. I extend Whitespeak with the notion of Whitespace—a discursive and psychic distance between matters of race and oppression. Whitespeak encompasses rhetorical methods of separating Whites from racism "through the subjecfication of race and racism, the erasure of agency, and the disembodiment of subjects" (p. 188). Whitespace is constructed and maintained through cultural artifacts, language, values, beliefs, and ideologies associated with White privilege and power.

Whitespace does not have to be expressed through language to be communicated effectively. Black communicators and other marginalized group members are almost always conscious of entering or exiting Whitespace, whereas Whites who take this space for granted may find it noticeable only when stepping outside its boundaries. Ultimately,

Whitespace may encourage or discourage, enable or constrain, and reveal or conceal race privilege at various levels. The social space is created and maintained through the ubiquitous and dynamic nature of Whiteness (Nakayama & Martin, 1999). To further attenuate the idea, I turn to another introspective narrative.

> Yesterday I attended a city council meeting. The reason for my attendance was to support six students who were arrested last Friday. I joined community members who came to voice their opinions concerning the mistreatment of the students. The arrests occurred outside a local bar. Reportedly the police arrived in response to a fight involving two White men. Some say the police began using abusive tactics against Black observers.
>
> The young men and women endured obscenities and were forced onto the hoods of patrol cars. One young man was shocked with a taser—a crowd control weapon that fires electric currents. The taser had not been used at the nearby block party, nor had a taser been used at a recent concert, although both events contained crowds much larger than the bar incident. The controversy continued into the next day when the six students were seen in jailhouse jumpsuits as they were being transferred between city buildings. The news traveled quickly through the small college town. The incident spurred questions about race.

The incident above occurred in a small college town in southeastern Ohio, where a substantial number of bars and restaurants contribute to a lively atmosphere for university students. On any given weekend students will engage in college fun. During holidays and special events, the festivities increase. Students fill the sidewalks with a sense of entitlement, and there appears to be little police interference. Also housed within the municipal area are the police department, city hall, and other businesses all separated by the distance of a short walk.

This university, like others, faces ongoing diversity challenges. At the time of the arrests, African American enrollment was less than 4%. The university and its surrounding business community serves a largely White population. Although multicultural events occur, the university and local establishments seem to cater less to international students and other people of color. Consequently, the town embodies very different spaces for different groups. Where some White students may find comfort and safety, other students may find discomfort. Exclusionary environments and alcohol never mix well; add feelings of indifference and the potential for intercultural conflict is intensified. Nevertheless, many students venture into town to celebrate the completion of final exams, birthdays, holidays, and just hang out. But some students cannot take for granted their entrance into Whitespace.

Arriving at City Hall, I joined three people in the elevator. I doubt anyone on that elevator was prepared for what we were about to encounter. When the doors opened the corridor was standing-room only. Every few minutes, the elevator doors would open and more people would join the crowd. Finally, a television was set up in the hallway. We watched the monitor and listened intently as the six students addressed the city council. Their words were powerful and sincere. They were upset and felt they had been the victims of racial profiling. They spoke not as troublemakers but as community members. Judging from the size of the crowd, their influence was obvious. Three of the young men claimed no prior arrests. One young woman had no prior experiences with law officers but now, admittedly, feared them. Another young woman cried. News about the issue had traveled beyond the city limits. An NAACP state branch representative promised that the organization's legal team would not rest until proper action had been taken. A representative from the Center for Institutional Equity spoke on behalf of the young men who had volunteered with her organization. The woman, who happened to be White, called for a new definition of the problem, "It's not an issue of sensitivity training and multiculturalism. Let's call it what it is—racism!"

The act of naming gives an issue a material semantic from which to build the conditions for dialogue. Making Whiteness visible is to stress personal perspective, adopt a spatial view of the assemblages of power relations, and re-articulate space as a counterhegemonic move. There is a need to identify how assemblages work and to analyze the rhetorical strategies that have historically secured the center as the place for Whites (Nakayama & Krizek, 1999). As illustrated through critical memory, rewriting history through an analysis of its constitutive rhetoric acknowledges the contributions of marginalized groups and validates the everyday practice and experience of those who have watched the center space of Whiteness from marginalized positions.

Returning to my example, a gaze had penetrated the city council. The veil had been lifted. As citizens stood before the microphone, the power of the spoken word called forth possibility that could not be ignored. These were the personal truths of the marginalized, supported by citizens who inhabit multiple spaces. One of the most forceful voices came from the White woman who had simply stated what many Blacks were thinking. Why did she feel entitled to speak without fear of repercussions? What power did she possess?

Knowledge and power are socially constructed rhetorical bodies (Foucault, 1972). As we have learned, rhetorical bodies occupy and simultaneously create spaces of power negotiations. Undoubtedly, the NAACP and the Center for Institutional Equity made a significant impact at the meeting. Each organization respectively challenged socio/histori-cal/political power. The organizational bodies united in opposition to oppression.

The discursive control of bodies is necessary for institutions to inscribe hierarchical relationships. The institutions in my example include the university, law enforcement, and the city council. Resistance came by way of individuals and organizations. Bodies of resistance include Blacks and Whites, students and professors, and community members who named and spoke out against racism. Although the six students had been victimized and perhaps terrorized for penetrating Whitespace, the council meeting served to express, represent and trans-form value for the multicultural other.

The next section elaborates my own Black masculinist standpoint. As a rhetorical body, I draw from previous examples of gaze, voice, and space in intercultural and interracial settings. By reversing the polarity of McIntosh's (1988) discussion, I present the reader with what have been, in my lived experience, common occurrences of denied privilege attributed to race and gender in dominant society.

MY BLACK MASCULINIST STANDPOINT
WITHIN WHITESPACE

African American men have historically felt the need to function with double-consciousness and negotiate cultural identity that is constantly in flux from one social position to another. From the Black boy to the invisible man, from Jeremiah Wright to Barack Obama—to be Black and male in America is an ongoing effort to avow identity.

Resistance for me is as much a struggle against rhetorical and phys-ical calamity as it is a struggle for gaze, voice, and space. Here I juxta-pose McIntosh's (1988) conception of privilege with my own lived expe-riences. Specifically, each statement reverses the polarity of privilege and re-articulates space from a marginalized perspective. I ask the reader to consider whether each "yes" represents a step toward privi-lege or denied-privilege:

- When my children are at school, I often wonder whether they will be treated fairly by staff and students, and whether race will be an issue.
- I can recall hearing one or more racist comments within the last week.
- There is rarely a time when race is not an issue in my social or professional life.
- Finding appropriate cultural products at local stores is never a sure thing.

- Wearing certain clothes and hairstyles come with the possibility of being subjected to stereotyping.
- In school, when learning about national heritage or civilization, there is a chance that my children will not hear about the ways in which people of color have contributed to it.
- Racial profiling is always a possibility, and I cannot be certain that law officers have my best interest at heart.
- When making decisions, I sometimes feel as though I am representing my race.
- My race and culture are not adequately represented in business, education, politics, and entertainment.
- When voicing concerns about racial issues at work or in class, I risk being regarded as overly sensitive and/or radical.
- I often ponder racist comments, for minutes, hours, and sometimes days.

Representations of race, gender, and space are exemplified in the sentiments above. By emphasizing my experience within Whitespace, I unmask the shifting dynamics of socially constituted power. Creating an appropriate and effective context in which to explore intercultural communication is a difficult challenge. Given that critical memory presents truth in the spirit of understanding, I hope these statements spark critical thoughts in the minds of readers. Whether readers agree or disagree is not the issue, for these are my own lived experiences. But the extent to which disagreement produces dialogue is very important. Racialized experiences impact my life but they do not define or represent the totality of my life. In the wake of recognizing and recording these tensions, I regain symbolic space and freedom.

Six

VOICE, GAZE, SPACE
AND WHY IT MATTERS

A Concluding Critical Memory
on the "Three Rules of Epidemics"

This chapter consists of two parts. First, I offer a final critical memory on matters of difference for the Black communicator. Next, I offer some concluding thoughts on the heuristic value of the ideas covered in this book.

DIFFUSING RACE AND GENDER
IN GLADWELL'S *THE TIPPING POINT*

Voice, space, and gaze inform interpretations of intercultural communication within every dimension of social life. Here, I examine intercultural incompetence at the nexus of health, academia, and popular culture. A critical-interpretive analysis of "Three Rules of Epidemics"—chapter 1 in Malcolm Gladwell's (2000) *The Tipping Point* reveals how Gladwell's discussion of sexually transmitted diseases simultaneously spreads inherently racist images of Black men. The analysis foregrounds ways in which Gladwell's representation of race, culture, and gender as diseased proves to be problematic for his subjects and readers alike.

> Tonight my class got into the Black–White thing again. And once again I felt the need to address my White peers by speaking on behalf of all Black people. This time, it began with a New York Times best-selling book that frames Black men as the primary cause of the world's sexually transmitted diseases. It is scary to think that people across the globe will read this crap. What's worse is that many readers believe it.

The previous paragraph was written when I was a graduate student. As one of a few Black men in a graduate program, I sometimes struggled with the arduous task of speaking on behalf of Black people. It is a dialectical tension, whether to address anything and everything having to do with my experience. I tried to balance speaking out with remaining silent, recognizing that both options come with a cost. Voicing one's disapproval can result in being labeled as sensitive or paranoid. Otherwise, I risk condoning racist perspectives with my silence. So one questions when, where, and how to speak for maximum results and minimum penalties. Strategic communication is necessary for success within the college classroom. In this case I chose to speak and then write truth into existence. The following section illustrates how I enact Black gaze and voice to oppose the problematic stereotype of Black men as epidemics.

A critical discussion of the "Three Rules of Epidemics"—chapter 1 in Malcolm Gladwell's (2000) *The Tipping Point*, reveals an amalgamation of racial and cultural stereotypes transmitted under the guise of scholarship. Building on fundamental assertions of diffusion theory (Rogers, 1995), Gladwell investigates three primary areas: the dispersion of messages and ideas; why some messages stick better than other messages; and the trends of societal behavior. Yet, in the process of his investigation, the author simultaneously disperses inherently racist images of Black men. Consequently, it is necessary to call attention to Gladwell's insidious construction of Black male identity, and the potent and popular misrepresentations of race, culture, and gender that prove harmful to Gladwell's subjects and readers alike.

The diffusion of innovation refers to implicit and explicit communication networks that operate on all societal levels (Rogers, 1995). Diffusion is the intentional and unintentional means by which a phenomenon spreads and/or becomes popular within society (e.g., messages, ideas, products, and, in this case—illness). Gladwell's (2000) *The Tipping Point* purports to explore the ways in which ideas, behaviors, and products infiltrate societal structures. The author claims to trace epidemics of illness, entertainment, and crime with the intent to answer two specific questions that lie at the heart of educators, parents, marketers, business people, and policymakers: Why is it that some ideas or behaviors or products start epidemics and others don't? And what can we do to deliberately start and control positive epidemics of our own? At the onset of his investigation, Gladwell's intent to better understand the spread of epidemics appears to be well served, considering how the diffusion of good ideas can contribute to social change. However, the author's discussion is problematic because of the racist constructs he draws from and diffuses in the process of his explication.

BLACK MEN AND DISEASE

Africa has long been represented as the birthplace of Acquired Immune Deficiency Syndrome (AIDS). Popular ideas about AIDS include cultural imaginings of African people as risk factors (Patton, 2002, p. xv). European scientists and scholars of the 20th century once suggested that "AIDS is probably the result of a new infection of human beings that began in central Africa, perhaps as recently as the 1950s" (Cantwell, 1988, p. 111). In addition, at one time the World Health Organization (WHO) linked sexually transmitted diseases to bio-attacks, extreme poverty, and hypersexual practices within African countries. Elsewhere, Dr. E. R. Fields blamed the rise of AIDS on Europe's importation of Blacks carrying the disease. Fields argued, "The spread of the AIDS virus to White females can clearly be laid at the feet of Negro bisexuals and Negro drug addicts" (Patton, 2002, p. 63). Undoubtedly, these mis-representations situate men of color as Black invaders, complete with infectious diseases.

SYPHILIS

Misinformed authors have attributed the spreading of sexually transmit-ted diseases to race and socioeconomic status in general, and to Black people specifically. In "Three Rules of Epidemics," Gladwell (2000) frames a syphilis epidemic in Baltimore, Maryland, as largely carried out by Black men who infect others through deviant sexual activity and drug dealing. Baltimore is an area densely populated by people of color, and Gladwell constructs his misrepresentation to support the notion that epidemics can be attributed to specific demographic and psycholog-ical profiles (e.g., physical and mental space). He writes, "Crack is known to cause a dramatic increase in the kind of risky sexual behavior that leads to the spread of things like HIV and syphilis" (Gladwell, 2000, p. 15). Furthermore, Gladwell's audience learns that such epidemics are caused by transmitters who come "into poor areas to buy drugs" (p. 15), poor people "who have experienced a breakdown in medical services" (p. 16), and the dislocated, described by the author as "these people" who were forced to "move to other parts of Baltimore, and who took their syphilis and other behaviors with them" (p. 17).

By stigmatizing individuals living in economically deprived areas, and neglecting to include denunciating references to those not residing in inner-city Baltimore, Gladwell attaches risky sexual behavior, syphilis, and other diseases to a specific demographic. For the uninformed reader, economic status and residence become the key criteria for deviance. Gladwell does not refer to race or ethnicity in his descriptions, but the message is clear because the author has primed the reader with examples of the people most likely to transmit syphilis. Thus, the uninformed reader is inundated with messages that implicate the Black male as the primary cause of America's battle with syphilis and other sexually transmitted diseases. To add, Gladwell (2000) quotes John Zenilman of Johns Hopkins University, who describes the disease as carried by a certain kind of person in Baltimore:

> [The disease is carried by a] very poor, probably drug-using, and sexually active individual. If that kind of person was suddenly transported from his or her old neighborhood to a new one—to a new part of town, where syphilis had never been a problem before—the disease would have an opportunity to tip. (p. 18)

Perhaps the aforementioned analogy is meant to support Gladwell's (2000) assertion that "in a given process, or system, some people matter more than others" (p. 19). Here, the reader is forced to inquire as to whom Gladwell is implicating in a societal system freighted with sexually transmitted disease.

HIV

Next, Gladwell addresses the Human Immunodeficiency Virus (HIV) epidemic by focusing on the largely Black community of East St. Louis, Missouri. The author claims that most epidemics can be attributed to less than 20% of any population, which would seem to admonish the potential for racial, cultural, and ethnic stereotyping. However, Gladwell presents the reader with another highly charged misrepresentation of Black men and women framed as drug dealers, child molesters, and prostitutes. Perhaps Gladwell's discussion relies on explicit descriptions of the presumed HIV transmitter as someone other than himself and his largely White audience. Gladwell asserts that HIV transmitters "aren't like you or me," and claims that transmitters can be found in the pool halls and roller-skating rinks of East St. Louis. These HIV carriers are given names and profiles that are supported by testimonies against them. For example, HIV embodied becomes one Darnell (Boss Man) McGee:

> He was big—over six feet—and charming, a talented skater, who wowed young girls with his exploits on the rink. His specialty was thirteen and fourteen-year-olds. He brought them jewelry, took them for rides in his Cadillac, got them high on crack, and had sex with them. (Gladwell, 2000, p. 20)

The image of a big Black man who seduces young girls as "his specialty" may symbolize reality for the uninformed reader with little to no knowledge or interaction with men of color. But perhaps Gladwell assumes that readers will independently reject such stereotypes.

As if the aforementioned descriptions were not enough, Gladwell continues to frame the stereotypical inner-city, HIV transmitter, by introducing a man identified as having worked the distressed downtown streets of Jamestown, New York. Nushawn Williams, also known as Face, Sly, or Shyteek, was, in the words of Gladwell (2000), a "Boss Man clone" who juggled women, apartments, drugs, and AIDS. The author adds that Williams "would buy his girlfriends roses, let them braid his long hair, and host all night marijuana and malt liquor-fueled orgies at his apartments" (p. 20). One might presume the image of the Cadillac—in the case of McGee, and braided hair and malt liquor—in the case of Williams, draw from popular characterizations of Black men. Regardless of the erroneousness, these stereotypes enforce epistemological assumptions in the minds of readers with little knowledge of Black men.

CRITICAL MEMORY
AND THE TUSKEGEE EXPERIMENT

Gladwell's (2000) deconstruction of the epidemic transmitter omits several pertinent, historical elements. For example, in his discussion of syphilis and Black men, the author neglects to mention the Tuskegee syphilis experiment where, between 1932 and 1972, the United States Public Health Service conducted an experiment on approximately 399 Black men in the late stages of syphilis (Jones, 1993). The men, largely sharecroppers from the poorest counties of Alabama, where told they were being treated for a blood illness, when in reality their doctors had no intention of curing them. Instead, these Black men were left to degenerate under the ravages of tertiary syphilis in the name of science—and spread the virus among their families in the process. Would this kind of experiment severely impact the diffusion of a virus among a demographic group? Has the critical memory of unethical medical practice contributed to mistrust of the dominant health care system?

Furthermore, Gladwell's (2000) investigations of the "exceptional people" who "drive social epidemics" (p. 21) include examples which do not parallel Boss Man McGee and Face Williams. Instead the author rhetorically represents White transmitters as much more human than Black America, which further perpetuates the intentional binary of race and gender. For example, when investigating the spread of pneumocystis carinii pneumonia (PCP) in the Dutch Providence of Limburg, Gladwell describes PCP as *somehow* infiltrating a Swedish Barrack. The epidemic is blamed on transfusions and un-sterilized needles rather than on the individuals themselves. Here, the uniformed reader is presented with images of an accidental epidemic spread among human beings, as opposed to that which is spread through the deviant actions of Blacks who are framed as less than human. To assert this position, Gladwell (2000) quotes the Dutch AIDS researcher, Jaap Goudmit:

> [The transmitter is] most likely at least one adult—probably a coal miner from Poland, Czechoslovakia, or Italy. . . . He could have transmitted the virus to his wife and offspring . . . unsterilized needles and syringes could have spread the virus. (p. 24)

In essence, the White man in the aforementioned quote is described as a working adult, with the responsibility of a wife and family; one who may have *accidentally* spread the virus, as opposed to Boss Man and Face—Black men who are seen as undeniably and intentionally spreading viruses.

Seemingly, Gladwell (2000) wants to understand how subliminal and unconscious messages impact societal members. For all intensive purposes he understands, yet he does not respect the danger in own message:

> We spend a lot of time thinking about how to make messages more contagious—how to reach as many people as possible with our products or ideas. . . . Stickiness means that a message makes an impact. You can't get it out of your head. (p. 25)

Gladwell's (2000) explication of the diffusion process imposes hegemonic misrepresentations of people of color, low income, and inner-city residents. Undoubtedly, all societal members must accept responsibility for their actions. No group is totally responsible for social dilemmas like syphilis and HIV. But to the uniformed reader, these stereotypes may represent some level of truth. In explicating the diffusion process, Gladwell's (2000) best-selling book diffuses racial and economic misperceptions to a wide audience, many of whom may not be unable to get these dangerously sticky messages out of their heads.

CONCLUSION:
FROM UNDERSTANDING TO ACTION

Encountering racism:
One reflection of numerous observations

Don't see it as wins or losses, victories or defeats
It, for lack of time and more accurate terms, is racism
Don't see it as neat, clean, and defined
It blurs between White and Black lines
For example, racism by proxy masks its face
And is not easily seen

Don't see it as wins or losses
Victories or defeats
Dealing with racism can get a little messy
Words run over, tears roll, voices lower and peak
Emotions apogee

You're in a space of pioneers
And you may be the first to have entered this place
So there are no guidelines per se
Only story, upon story, upon story. . .

So speak, and, in the words of Dianne Reeves:
Be kind to yourself/ be proud of yourself/
Love yourself/ support yourself/ respect yourself/
And know yourself

Speak not in terms of wins or losses
Or victories and defeats
But in terms of carving out space for the next person
And if you choose not to speak
That's OK too. There will be other times

—Hopson (2005)

In concluding this book, I call for increased efforts to understand the ways in which race and culture impact communication. At the risk of being prescriptive, I encourage readers to examine their own communicative practices for the purpose of acquiring and acting on new knowledge. Intercultural communication is a collective endeavor, but we each see, speak, and feel it differently. For example, up to this point I have opened myself to readers. Now I present the reader with these rhetorical questions: How have you enacted communication in dimensions of gaze, voice, and space? Are there other dimensions you would explore? What have you contributed to the communication process?

Culture can reflect race, region, gender, social class, and any symbolic system (Collier & Thomas, 1988). We interact as cultural bodies representing assorted values, beliefs, practices, and ideologies. We transmit one or more of these elements during communication. Intentional or otherwise, societies privilege some cultural groups while denying privilege to others, to the point of ethnocentrism. Words take on multiple meanings in the hegemonic space of ethnocentricity. The following are comments I have heard in the classroom:

> "That's just the way things are."
> "Things aren't that bad."
> "We're all the same."
> "Blacks can't contribute to racism."
> "Sure racism exists but that has nothing to do with me."
> "I just ignore it."

The ethnocentric mindset is limited by perceptions of one's own truth as right and all other truths as wrong. Based on tenets of isolation and separation, the ethnocentric mindset denies difference, defends against difference, and minimizes difference. Within the continuum of ethnocentricity, other cultural truths are seen as threatening or ignored until they become virtually invisible. For example, one might choose to overlook or disregard my Black communicative experience. Indeed, McIntosh (1988) could have chosen to ignore her own experiences with White privilege.

On the other hand, the ethnorelative mindset is sensitive to how and why difference matters. Here, one recognizes and accepts other interpretations of the world, and works within the idea of multiple truths as opposed to trying to eliminate them. In addition, one adapts to new ways of thinking and transforms knowledge into cultural currency. Most importantly, moving into a space of responsibility requires action as defined by the individual. No two situations or people are identical. Healthy intercultural communication is not achieved through prescription. However, some of my students have used words which, I think, exemplify a good start:

> "I attend as many different cultural events as possible."
> "When I'm not sure about something, I ask."
> "Everyone has culture worth sharing."
> "I'm not sure why you feel that way. Please help me understand."
> "Beyond different bodies, true diversity requires commitment, work, and resources."

These statements extend Bennett's (1993) framework for intercultural sensitivity development. Between the lines are examples of self-reflexivity, empathy, acceptance, adaptability, and action. The statements contribute to a theoretical space suitable for explicating communication and power. These students have made the leap from insensitivity to responsibility.

This book intentionally blurred the lines of past and present. I aligned, superimposed, and knotted together yesterday and today in order to contribute to discussions about Black communication and intercultural communication. I began by asking how Black communication within the United States becomes an intercultural experience. In my exploration, Black communication is a unique form of intercultural communication because the historical and current discursive practices of Black Americans are forged in the crucible of tension and strategy, and produced and maintained within a predominantly White societal structure. As we see in the texts of Ellison (1952), hooks (1996), and Wright (1945), the synoptic story of the Black experience is expressed over myriad times and tongues. Multiple messages recounting that vexed experience are imparted through a mixture of narratives, songs, sermons, and stories—all of which have a significant place in intercultural communication research.

The second guiding question concerned the distinctive truths of Black communication, and the specific tensions and strategies associated with these truths. By placing critical memory within an intercultural context I found that Black communicators speak largely to ways in which race and racism contribute to dialectical tensions of the Black self as good–bad, visible–invisible, voice–voiceless, and empowered–disempowered. To address these tensions, Black communicators may strategically silence themselves, confront their oppressors, gain trust from others, and educate others. In addition, some communicators demonstrate double consciousness across dimensions of gaze, voice, and space.

My final research question addressed African American rhetorical traditions that work to express, represent, and transform Black life. Using critical memory to frame a unique communication phenomenon, I highlighted the ways in which some communicators employ nommo to name, resist, redefine, and rearticulate the nonmonolithic Black experience. These texts qualify as communication channels. The talking drum resounds across generations. Black communicators continue to rely on the rhetoric of reaffirmation and possibility, and language lends to alternative forms of organizing space. Moreover, our survival calls for profound optimism, ongoing imperatives to overcome racism, and creative mediums to theorizing the human journey. Tradition lives on in stories and songs of today. Art, music, poetry, writing, and yes, academic works are essential to freedom. I believe that scholarly investigations should contribute to and interrogate everyday life. The intrinsic nature of intercultural communication research includes the articulation of that experience.

I hope to meet two valuable objectives with this book. First, I want to inspire thought concerning the inclusion or omission of human experiences. Reflection encourages dialogue. Assorted stories bring new truths to light. The more we listen, the more we begin to care about our intercultural relationships. If I have been successful you will consider additional questions and projects related to intercultural communication. Competence is achieved through cultivated knowledge, changed mindsets, and increased awareness.

I did not claim to speak for or about all people. The ideas espoused here are based in subjective truths, not universal truth. And yet, I do not underestimate the book's potential to connect with someone's experience and/or desire for consciousness-raising. A common land, language, or classroom does not justify one culture. To be fair, my observations of difference, culture, and power move beyond Black communities. Scholarly perspectives should target communicative practices and cultural power imbalances wherever they take place. Understanding any sociohistorical context requires that we explicate its manifold of layers. In doing so, we may begin to understand what Y. Y. Kim (2004) describes as the relatively high degrees of difference and the process in which communicators of vexed cultural backgrounds come into direct contact with one another.

My second objective is to foreground the communicative tensions and strategies of societal group members whose views have been excluded from the annals of academic inquiry. I challenge assumptions of what experiences constitute knowledge. Academia claims to be open to new knowledge, but I have spent my share of time in classrooms, meetings, conferences, and so on, and I know what it is to be the outsider-within (Hill Collins, 1990). As such I have a great appreciation for opportunities to explicate power more thoroughly. I regard communication as liberation. According to Shakur (2001), the less you think about oppression, the more your tolerance for it grows. After a while, people just think oppression is the normal state of things. But to become free, you have to be acutely aware of being a slave.

Finally, I hope readers will build on strengths and forgive any shortcomings associated with this project. My discussion focused specifically on interactions among U.S. Blacks and Whites, but a wide range of intercultural and interracial experiences exist in this nation and across the globe. Countless stories await study. Making sense of the human experience requires adequate representations of multiple experiences. I chose to begin with my talking drum. Adhering to the way of Maat, I will continue to work at bringing good into the world.

Communication II

The Student

> The dust of ancient pages
> had never touched his face
> and fountains Black and comely
> were mummyfied in a place
> beyond
> his young un-knowing.

The Teacher

> She shared the lettered strivings
> of etched Pharaonic walls
> and reconstruction's anguish
> resounded down the halls
> of all her
> dry dreams.

> —Maya Angelou (1986)

REFERENCES

Abel, E., Christian, B., & Moglen, H. (1997). *Female subjects in Black and White*. Berkeley: University of California Press.

Akbar, N. (1985). *The community of self*. Tallahassee, FL: Mind Productions and Associates.

Alkebulan, A. (2003). The spiritual essence of African American rhetoric. In R. L. Jackson & E. B. Richardson (Eds.), *Understanding African American rhetoric: Classical origins to contemporary innovations* (pp. 23–40). New York: Routledge.

Allen, B. J. (1996). Feminist standpoint theory: A Black woman's review of organizational socialization. *Communication Studies, 47*, 257–271.

Als, H. (2001). The shop. In I. Ebong (Ed.), *Black hair: Art, style, culture* (pp. 52–64). New York: Universe Publishing.

America's Promise Alliance Report. (2008). www.americaspromise.org/Research-and-Reports/c/Cities-in-Crisis-2008.aspx

Angelou, M. (1986). *Maya Angelou: Poems*. New York: Bantam Books.

Asante, M. K. (1998). *The afrocentric idea*. Philadelphia, PA: Temple University Press.

Asante, M. K. (2003). The future of African American rhetoric. In R. L. Jackson & E. B. Richardson (Eds.), *Understanding African American rhetoric: Classical origins to contemporary innovations*. New York: Routledge.

Asim, J. (2007). *The "N" word*. New York: Houghton Mifflin.

Awkward, M. (2000). A Black man's place in Black feminist criticism. In J. James & T. D. Sharpeley-Whiting (Eds.), *The Black feminist reader* (pp. 88–108). Malden, MA: Blackwell Publishers.

Back, L., & Solomos, J. (2000). *Theories of race and racism: A reader.* London: Routledge.

Baker, H. (2001). *Critical memory: Public spheres, African American writing and Black fathers and sons in America.* Athens: The University of Georgia Press.

Baldwin, J., & Meade, M. (1971/1992). *A rap on race.* New York: Laurel Leaf.

Banks, I. (2000). *Hair matters: Beauty, power, and Black women's consciousness.* New York: New York University Press.

Bennett, L. (1968). *Before the Mayflower: The history of the Negro in America, 1619–1964.* Baltimore, MD: Pelican Books.

Bennett, M. J. (1993). Towards ethnorelativism: A developmental model of intercultural sensitivity. In R. M. Paige (Ed.), *Education for the intercultural experience* (pp. 21–71). Yarmouth, ME: Intercultural Press.

Bennett, M., & Dickerson, V. D. (2001). *Recovering the Black female body.* New Brunswick, NJ: Rutgers.

Berger, P. L., & Luckmann, T. (1967). *The social construction of reality: A treatise in the sociology of knowledge.* New York: First Anchor Books.

Boylorn, R. (2008). As seen on TV: A Black woman's reflection on race and reality television. *Critical Studies in Media Communication, 25*(4), 413–433.

Brown, E. (1992). *A taste of power: A Black woman's story.* New York: HarperCollins Publishers.

Byrd, A., & Tharps, L. L. (2001). *Hair story. Untangling the roots of Black hair in America.* New York: St. Martin's Press.

Cantwell, A. R. (1988). *AIDS & the doctors of death: An inquiry into the origin of the AIDS epidemic.* Los Angeles, CA: Aries Rising Press.

Carter, B., & Steinberg, J. (2007, April 13). Off the air: The lights go out for Don Imus. *The New York Times,* p. C1.

Chopra, D. (1994). *The seven spiritual laws of success.* San Rafael, CA: Amber-Allen Publishing.

Christian, B. (1985). *Black feminist criticism: Perspectives on Black women writers.* Elmsford, NY: Pergamon Press.

Collier, M. J. (2000). *Constituting cultural difference through discourse.* Thousand Oaks, CA: Sage.

Collier, M. J., & Thomas, M. (1988). Cultural identity: An interpretive perspective. In Y. Y. Kim & W. B. Gudykunst (Eds.), *Theories in intercultural communication.* Thousand Oaks, CA: Sage.

Cooley, C. (1902). *Human nature and the social order.* New York: Scribner's Publishing.

Cooper, J. C. (1994). *The matter is life.* New York: Doubleday Publishing.

Cress Welsing, F. (1991). *The Isis (Yssis) papers.* Chicago, IL: Third World Press.

Cummings J. N. (2000). When Miss America was always White. In A. Gonzalez, M. Houston, & V. Chen (Eds.), *Our voices: Essays in culture, ethnicity, and communication* (pp. 42–46). Los Angeles, CA: Roxbury.

Dandy, E. B. (1991). *Black communications: Breaking down the barriers*. Chicago, IL: African American Images.

Davis, J., Muhammad, A., Taylor, M., & Hubbard, F. (1993). "Sucka nigga." Recorded by A Tribe Called Quest. On *Midnight Marauders* [audio recording]. New York: Jive/BMG Records.

Delgado, R., & Stefancic, J. (2001). *Critical race theory*. New York: New York Press.

DeVeaux, A. (1987). *An enchanted hair tale*. New York: HarperTrophy.

Douglass, F. (1970). The life of Frederick Douglass. In W. Adams, P. Conn, & B. Slepian (Eds.), *Afro American literature* (pp. 3–8). Boston, MA: Houghton Mifflin Company.

Du Bois, W. E. B. (1897/2004). The conservation of races. In P. Zuckerman (Ed.), *The social theory of W. E. B. DuBois* (pp. 19–23). Thousand Oaks, CA: Pine Forge Press.

Du Bois, W. E. B. (1903/1999). *The souls of Black folk*. New York: W. W. Norton & Company.

Dyer, M. (1997). *White*. New York: Routledge.

Dyer, R. (2000) The matter of Whiteness. In L. Back & J. Solomos (Eds.), *Theories of race and racism: A reader* (pp. 539–548). New York: Routledge.

Ebong, I. (2001). *Black hair: Art, style, culture*. New York: Universe Publishing.

Ellison, R. (1952). *Invisible man*. New York: Random House.

Entz, G. R. (2003). Benjamin "Pap" Singleton: Father of the Kansas Exodus. In N. Mjagkij (Ed.), *Portraits of African American life since 1865* (pp. 15–34). Wilmington DE: Scholarly Resources Inc.

Eskew, G. T. (1997). 'Bombingham': Black protest in postwar Birmingham, Alabama. *Historian, 59*(2), 371–390.

Fanon, F. (1967). *Black skin, White masks: The experiences of a Black man in a White world*. New York: Grove Press.

Fanon, F. (2000). The fact of Blackness. In L. Back & J. Solomos (Eds.), *Theories of race and racism: A reader* (pp. 257–266). New York: Routledge.

Foucault, M. (1972). *The archaeology of knowledge & discourse on language*. New York: Harper Colophon Books.

Foucault, M. (1980). *Power/knowledge: Selected interviews and other writings, 1972–77*. New York: Pantheon.

Frankenburg, R. (2000). White woman, race matters: The social construction of Whiteness. In L. Back & J. Solomos (Eds.), *Theories of race and racism: A reader* (pp. 447–461). New York: Routledge.

Fuller, N. (1984). *The united independent compensatory code/system/concept: A textbook/workbook for thought, speech, and/or action for victims of racism (White supremacy)*. Unknown binding.

Gauntlett, D. (2002). *Media, gender, and identity*. New York: Routledge.

Gibson, N. C. (2003). *Fanon: The postcolonial imagination*. Cambridge, UK: Polity Press.

Gilroy, P. (1993). *The Black Atlantic: Modernity and double consciousness*. Cambridge, MA: Harvard University Press.

Gladwell, M. (2000). *The tipping point: How little things make a big difference*. New York: Little, Brown and Company.

Gonzalez, A., Houston, M., & Chen, V. (2004). *Our voices: Essays in culture, ethnicity, and communication*. Los Angeles, CA: Roxbury Publishing.

Gray, C. C. (2001). *Afrocentric thought and praxis: An intellectual history*. Trenton, NJ: African World Press.

Gudykunst, W. B., & Kim, Y. Y. (1992). *Readings on communicating with strangers: An approach to intercultural communication*. New York: McGraw-Hill.

Hacker, A. (1992). *Two nations: Black and White, separate, hostile, unequal*. New York: Charles Scribner's.

Hall, S. (2003). The Whites of their eyes: Racist ideologies and the media. In G. Dines & J. M. Humez (Eds.), *Gender, race, and class in the media* (pp. 89–93). Thousand Oaks, CA: Sage.

Hasian, M. A., & Nakayama, T. K. (1998). The fictions of racialized identities. In J. M. Sloop & J. M. McDaniel (Eds.), *Judgment calls, politics, and indeterminacy* (pp. 182–195). Boulder, CO: Westview Press.

Hecht, M. L., Jackson, R. L., & Ribeau, S. A. (2003). *African American communication: Exploring identity and culture*. Mahwah, NJ: Lawrence Erlbaum Associates.

Heilemann, J., & Halperin, M. (2010). *Game change: Obama and the Clintons, McCain and Palin, and the race of a lifetime*. New York: HarperCollins.

Herron, C. (1997). *Nappy hair*. New York: Knopf.

Hill Collins, P. (1990). *Black feminist thought: Knowledge, consciousness, and the politics of empowerment*. New York: HarperCollins.

Hine, D. C., Hine, W. C., & Harrold, S. (2003). *The African American odyssey*. Upper Saddle River, NJ: Pearson Education Company.

hooks, b. (1992). Whiteness in the black imagination. In L. Grossberg, C. Nelson, & P. Treichler (Eds.), *Cultural studies* (pp. 338–346). New York: Routledge.

hooks, b. (1996). *Bone Black: Memories of girlhood*. New York: Henry Holt.

hooks, b. (1999a). *Happy to be nappy*. New York: Hyperion Books for Children.

hooks, b. (1999b). Excerpts from feminist theory: From margin to center. In K. Foss, S. Foss, & C. L. Griffin (Eds.), *Feminist rhetorical theories* (pp. 69–99). Thousand Oaks, CA: Sage.

Hopson, M. C. (2005) *The talking drum: Critical memory in intercultural communication research*. Unpublished dissertation. Athens: Ohio University.

Hopson, M. C. (2007). Negotiations of organizational Whitespace. Critical reflections of power, privilege, and intercultural (in)sensitivity within academia. In B. J. Allen, L. Flores, & M. P. Orbe (Eds.), *International and intercultural communication annual: Communication within/across organizational contexts* (Vol. XXX). Washington, DC: National Communication Organization.

Hopson, M. C. (2009). Language and girlhood: Conceptualizing Black feminist thought in "Happy to be Nappy." *Women and Language, 32*(1).

Houston, M., & Davis, O. (2002). *Centering ourselves: African American feminist and womanist studies of discourse*. Cresskill, NJ: Hampton Press.

Howell, D. W. (2004a). *I was a slave: True life stories as dictated by former American slaves in the 1930s. The lives of slave women*. Washington, DC: American Legacy Books.

Howell, D. W. (2004b). *I was a slave: True life stories as dictated by former American slaves in the 1930s. The lives of slave men*. Washington, DC: American Legacy Books.

Jackson, R. L., & Hopson, M. C. (in press). *Race, gender, communication, and Black men in the 21st century*. New York: Peter Lang Publishing.

James, J., & Sharpley-Whiting. T. D. (2000). *The Black feminist reader*. Malden, MA: Blackwell Publishers.

Johnson, C., & McCluskey, J. (1997). *Black men speaking*. Bloomington: Indiana University Press.

Jones, J. H. (1993). *Bad blood: The Tuskegee syphilis experiment*. New York: The Free Press.

Karenga, M. (2003). Nommo, Kawaida and communicative practice: Bringing good into the world. In R. L. Jackson & E. B. Richardson (Eds.), *Understanding African American rhetoric: Classical origins to contemporary innovations* (p. 322). New York: Routledge.

Kellner, D. (2003). Cultural studies, multiculturalism, and media culture. In G. Dines & J. M. Humez (Eds.), *Gender, race, and class in the media* (pp. 126–132). Thousand Oaks, CA: Sage.

Kim, Y. Y. (2004). Long term cross-cultural adaptation. In D. Landis, J. M. Bennett, & M. J. Bennett (Eds.), *Handbook of intercultural training*. Thousand, Oaks, CA: Sage Publications.

Kochman, T. (1981). *Black and white styles in conflict*. Chicago, IL: University of Chicago Press.

Kunjufu, K. (1986). *Countering the conspiracy to destroy Black boys, Vol. II*. Chicago, IL: African American Images.

Landis, D., Bennett, J. M., & Bennett, M. J. (2004) *Handbook of intercultural training*. Thousand Oaks, CA: Sage.

Lee, S., & Pollard, S. D. (1997). *4 little girls* [documentary film]. New York: HBO.

Lynn, L. (2000). "Song for Assata." On *"Like water for chocolate"* (audio recording). New York: Geffen Records.

Martin, J. N., & Davis, O. I. (2001). Conceptual foundations for teaching about Whiteness in intercultural communication courses. *Communication Education, 50*(4), 1-25.

Martin, J. N., & Nakayama, T. K. (1999). Thinking dialectically about culture and communication. *Communication Theory, 9*(1), 1–25.

Marty, D. (1999). White antiracist rhetoric as apologia: Wendell Berry's "The hidden wound." In T. K. Nakayama & J. Martin (Eds.), *Whiteness: The communication of social identity* (pp. 51–68). Thousand Oaks, CA: Sage.

McCracken, G. (1988). *The long interview*. Newbury Park, CA: Sage.

McKay, C. (1928/2003) Home to Harlem. In D. C. Hine, W. C. Hine, & S. Harold (Eds.), *The African American Odyssey*. Upper Saddle River, NJ: Pearson Education Company.

McKerrow, R. E. (1998). Corporeality and cultural rhetoric: A site for rhetoric's future. *Southern Communication Journal, 63*, 315–328.

McIntosh, P. (1988). *White privilege: Unpacking the invisible knapsack.* Retrieved on September 11, 2003, from http://www.Utoronto.ca/acc/ events/peggy1.htm.

McPhail, M. (2003). The politics of (in)visibility in African American rhetorical scholarship. A (re)quest for an African worldview. In. R. L. Jackson & E. B. Richardson (Eds.), *Understanding African American rhetoric: Classical origins to contemporary innovations* (pp. 99–113). New York: Routledge

Means Coleman, R. (2002). *Say it loud!: African American audiences, media, and identity.* New York: Routledge.

Metress, C. (2002). *The lynching of Emmett Till: A documentary narrative.* Charlottesville: The University of Virginia Press.

Moody, A. (1970). The movement. In W. Adams, P. Conn, & B. Slepian (Eds.), *Afro-American literature* (pp. 109–116). Boston, MA: Houghton Mifflin.

Moon, D. (1999). White enculturation and bourgeois ideology: The discursive production of good white girls. In T. K. Nakayama & J. N. Martin (Eds.), *Whiteness: The communication of social identity.* Thousand Oaks, CA: Sage.

Muhammad, N. (2000). Definitions of the educational battlefield. Unpublished document. Athens: Ohio University.

Nakayama, T. K., & Krizek, R. L. (1999). Whiteness as strategic rhetoric. In T. K. Nakayama & J. N. Martin (Eds.), *Whiteness: The communication of social identity* (p. 105). Thousand Oaks, CA: Sage.

Nakayama, T. K., & Martin, J. N. (1999) *Whiteness: The communication of social identity.* Thousand Oaks, CA: Sage.

Northup, S. (1968). *Twelve years a slave.* Baton Rouge: Louisiana State University Press.

Nunnelly, W.A. (1991). *Bull Connor.* Tuscaloosa: University of Alabama Press.

Odih, P. (2002). Mentors and role models: Masculinity and the educational underachievement of young Afro-Caribbean males. *Race, Ethnicity, and Education, 5*(1), 92–105.

Orbe, M. P. (1998). *Constructing co-cultural theory: An explication of culture, power, and communication.* Thousand Oaks, CA: Sage.

Orbe, M. P., & Harris, T. M. (2001). *Interracial communication: Theory into practice.* Stamford, CT: Thomson Learning.

Owen, W. (1984). Interpretive themes in relational communication. *Quarterly Journal of Speech, 70,* 274–287.

Patton, C. (2002). How to have theory in an epidemic: Cultural chronicles of AIDS. *International Journal of Epidemiology, 31*, 500–501.

Payne, R. (2001). *A framework for understanding poverty.* Highlands, TX: Aha Process Inc.

Potkay, A., & Burr, S. (1995). *Black Atlantic writers of the eighteenth century.* New York: St. Martin's Press.

Rogers, E. M. (1995). *Diffusion of innovations.* New York: The Free Press.

Rooks, N. (2001). Wearing your hair wrong: Hair, drama, and a politics of representation for African American women at play on a battlefield. In M. Bennett & V. D. Dickerson (Eds.), *Recovering the Black female body: Self representation by African American women* (pp. 279–295). New Brunswick, NJ: Rutgers University Press.

Scott, J. (2004). "Still here." On *Beautifully human* (audio recording). New York: Hidden Beach Recordings.

Shakur, A. (2001). *Assata: An autobiography.* New York: Lawrence Hill Books.

Smitherman, G. (2000). *Talkin' that talk: Language, culture, and education in African America.* New York: Routledge.

Sokolowski, R. (2000). *Introduction to phenomenology.* Cambridge, UK: Cambridge University Press.

Spellers, R. E. (2002). Happy to be nappy: Embracing an Afrocentric aesthetic for beauty. In J. N. Martin, T. K. Nakayama, & L. A. Flores (Eds.), *Readings in intercultural communication: Experiences and contexts* (pp. 52–59). Boston, MA: McGraw-Hill.

Stage, C. (1999). We celebrate 100 years: An indigenous analysis of the metaphors that shape the cultural identity of Small Town, USA. In T. K. Nakayama & J. N. Martin (Eds.), *Whiteness: The communication of social identity* (pp. 69–85). Thousand Oaks, CA: Sage.

Staples, R. (1998). *Black masculinity: The Black man's role in American society.* San Francisco, CA: Black Scholar Books.

Taylor, Y. (2005). *Growing up in slavery: Stories of young slaves as told by themselves.* Chicago, IL: Lawrence Hill Books.

Toure, S. (1969). A dialectical approach to culture. *The Black Scholar, 1*(1), 11–26.

Truth, S. (1850/1998). *Narrative of Sojourner Truth: A bondswoman of olden time with a history of her labors and correspondence.* New York: Penguin Books.

Tutu, D. (2004). *God has a dream: A vision of hope for our time.* New York: Doubleday.

Walker, A. (1983). *In search of our mothers' gardens: Womanist prose.* Orlando FL: Harcourt Brace & Company.

Warfield-Coppock, N. (1990). *Afrocentric theory and applications, Vol. I: Adolescent rites of passage.* Washington, DC: Baobab Associates, Inc.

West, C. (1993). *Race matters.* Boston, MA: Beacon.

Williams, R. (1972). *The BITCH Test (Black intelligence test of cultural homogeneity).* St. Louis, MO: Washington University, Black Studies Program.

Woodson, C. G. (1933/1990). *Mis-education of the Negro.* Nashville, TN: Winston-Derek.

Woodyard, J. (2003). Africological theory and criticism: Reconceptualizing communication constructs. In R. L. Jackson & E. B. Richardson (Eds.), *Understanding African American rhetoric: Contemporary origins to contemporary innovations* (pp. 153–154). New York: Routledge.

Wright, R. (1945). *Black boy: A record of childhood and youth.* New York: Harper & Row.

wsj.com/washwire/2008/10/07/obama-campaign-takes-issue-with-mccains-
    that-one-remark
Yarbrough, C. (1979). *Cornrows*. New York: The Putnam & Grosset Group.

ADDITIONAL READING

Bennett, J. M. (1993). Cultural marginality: Identity issues in intercultural training. In M. Bennett (Ed.), *Education for the multicultural experience* (pp. 99–120). Yarmouth, ME: Intercultural Press, Inc.

Boyd, H. (2000). *Autobiography of a people: Three centuries of African American history told by those who lived it*. New York: DoubleDay.

Crawley, R. L. (1999). *Always on display: An interpretive exploration of the essence of the African American male experience at a predominantly White university*. Unpublished dissertation. Athens: Ohio University.

Delpit, L. (2001) Ebonics and culturally responsive instruction: What should teachers do? In B. Bigelow, B. Harvey, S. Karp, & L. Miller (Eds.), *Rethinking our classrooms: Teaching for equity and justice* (pp. 22–25). Williston, VA: A Rethinking Schools Publication.

Dillard, J. L. (1973). *Black English: Its history and usage in the United States*. New York: Vintage Books.

Diop, C. A. (1989). *The African origins of civilization: Myth or reality?* New Brunswick, NJ: Transaction books, *Journal of African Civilizations*.

Fanon, F. (1963). *The wretched of the earth*. New York: Grove Press.

Foucault M. (1995). *Discipline and punishment: The birth of the prison*. New York: Vintage Books.

Gates, H. L. (1988). *Signifying monkey*. New York: Oxford University Press.

Griffin, E. (2000). *Communication: A first look at communication theory*. Boston, MA: McGraw-Hill.

Hopson, M. C. (2000). *Soul searching: Portrait of a young Black man.* Grand Rapids, MI: HPC.

Hopson, M. C. (2001). Observations of DWB: A very real issue. *The Journal of Intergroup Relations, 28*(3), 77–80.

Houston, M. (2004, November). *Introducing Patricia Hill-Collins.* Unpublished presentation at the annual meeting of the National Communication Association, Chicago, IL.

Jackson, R. L. (2006). *Scripting the Black masculine body: Identity, discourse, and racial politics in popular media.* Albany: State University of New York Press.

Langellier, K. (1989). Personal narratives: Perspectives on theory and research. *Text and Performance Quarterly, 9,* 243–276.

Martin, J. N., Nakayama, T. K., & Flores, L. A. (2002). *Readings in intercultural communication: Experiences and contexts.* Boston, MA: McGraw-Hill.

Mjagkij, N. (2003). *Portraits of African American life since 1865.* Wilmington, DE: Scholarly Resources.

Muhammad, N. (2004). *On history.* Unpublished essay. Athens: Ohio University

Pusch, M. (2004). Intercultural training in historical perspective. In D. Landis, J. M. Bennett, & M. J. Bennett (Eds.), *Handbook of intercultural training* (pp. 219–226). Thousand Oaks, CA. Sage.

Samovar, L. A., & Porter, R. E. (2001). *Communication between cultures.* Belmont, CA: Wadsworth.

Shome, R. (1999). Whiteness and the politics of location. In T. K. Nakayama & J. N. Martin (Eds.), *Whiteness: The communication of social identity* (pp. 107–128). Thousand Oaks, CA: Sage.

Singhal, A., & Rogers, E. M. (1999). *Entertainment education: A communication strategy for social change.* Mahwah, NJ: Lawrence Erlbaum Associates.

Smitherman, G. (2002). Foreword. In M. Houston & O. Davis (Eds.), *Centering ourselves.* Cresskill, NJ: Hampton Press.

Wood, J. T. (2004). *Communication: Theories in action.* Belmont, CA: Wadsworth/Thomson Learning.

AUTHOR INDEX

SUBJECT INDEX

CPSIA information can be obtained
at www.ICGtesting.com
Printed in the USA
FFOW03n1758010217
31966FF